COMING
ABOUT

COMING ABOUT

LIFE IN THE BALANCE

MARIO DELL'OLIO

While every precaution has been taken in the preparation of this book, the publisher assumes no responsibility for errors or omissions, or for damages resulting from the use of the information contained herein.

COMING ABOUT
First edition. May 20, 2018.
Copyright © 2018 Mario Dell'Olio

ISBN: 978-0-692-12078-1

"To Jim, whose presence at my side during each trial and each life threatening moment gave me the strength to persevere, to never give up. We will never drift apart."

PART I

THE

DREAM

CHAPTER
1

The waves were crashing all around me, pushing me further away from the boat. My vision was obscured by the relentless onslaught of white water assaulting me from every direction. I frantically kicked my legs to stay above the surface of the seemingly bottomless ocean. The shoreline was miles away, and I trembled in fear. I struggled to catch my breath as wave after wave struck my face. The taste of the salty sea scorched my already dehydrated mouth. I reached in vain for the white plastic garbage bag that was being tossed around like a beach ball in the surf. It contained all of the crucial documents that I had salvaged – I had to get hold of it.

It was difficult to distinguish the shiny plastic from the white frothy foam of the crashing waves. The bag was almost within my grasp when I was suddenly pulled under. I was disoriented, submerged beneath the tumbling waters. The din of the violent waves was thunderous. I was terrified as I fought against the force of the surf that pushed and twisted my already weakened body. Resisting the impulse to panic, I battled my way back to the top. I needed air. I gathered my remaining strength and propelled myself through the tumult. I pierced the surface and gasped as oxygen filled my burning lungs.

Letting go of the boat to retrieve that plastic bag had been foolish. I was in the midst of the turbulent waters of the coral reef without a life jacket, fighting to stay afloat. I had lost sight of the bag and was desperately scanning for it when it popped up after having been submerged. This time I managed to grab hold of it. At least we had our passports and the little cash we had brought with us. But at that moment, I felt no relief. Rather, a wave of irrepressible anger welled up within me as I looked up at the gray sky. "What the hell have you done to us?" I screamed.

It was an incredibly irrational response to the circumstances I found myself in. I didn't cry or even feel particularly relieved. Instead, I erupted in anger towards God. How could He have let this happen to us? My worst nightmare was coming true. We were miles from the shore, getting pummeled into the coral reefs. My body began to shake as I felt my childhood fear of the open ocean welling to the surface. Would we survive? Barely keeping my head above water, I used my free arm to battle my way back to the dinghy, all the while seething with anger.

How did we end up here? What possessed us to leave San Francisco? We had successful jobs, a beautiful home, and a community of friends whom we loved. The plans we had for our future were grand. We traveled extensively, and every country we visited held some allure. We would fantasize about what it would be like to live in Italy or Ireland or Spain. I'd joke about leaving it all behind and starting a new adventure in some far-away location. On our most recent vacation, the beauty of the Caribbean had seduced us. The sun's rays sparkled on the clear blue water. Sailing from island to island and feeling the warm breeze caress our faces, there seemed to be no downside to living in that part of the world. After years of fantasizing about retiring in an exotic destination, we took a leap of faith.

Now our survival hung in the balance as we fought for our lives in the beautiful waters that had drawn us to the Caribbean. Their beauty had beguiled us to leave everything behind in order to live in a tropical paradise. How could it all have gone so wrong?

CHAPTER 2

It was December 2000, and we had everything we could have wanted. Our condo was an expansive five-bedroom unit on two-and-a-half floors, between Noe Valley and the Castro district in San Francisco. Our deck and family living area had breathtaking views of downtown and the Bay Bridge. The neighborhood was great, with coffee shops and restaurants within a short walking distance. Jim had been an interior designer during his previous career in Washington, D.C., so every room had its own distinct atmosphere. One of his signature designs was the use of bold, deep colors on both ceilings and walls. Our dining room walls were painted a deep cherry with a lavender ceiling. The master bedroom had royal blue walls and a military tan ceiling.

One of the best features of the condo was the beautiful roof deck between the second and third levels. We had built the deck ourselves using bowed copper tubing from the plumbing section of Home Depot as railings. They were bent at each redwood post, which created a semi-circular edge rather than a straight one. We planted a red maple and two lemon trees in huge pots, and there were flowers, tomatoes, and numerous herbs and spices growing. It was an incredible home in a beautiful and sunny neighborhood.

Our lives together were in total contrast to my first years in San Francisco. I had driven cross-country with a colleague from the high school where I taught in Connecticut. Sean and I were both embarking on major life-changing journeys; he was to return to the east coast to start law school, and I would remain in San Francisco to begin my new life. I moved into a nice little apartment with a roommate I had only met through phone conversations. My full-time job at Mission Dolores Basilica paid $16,000 in 1990, so those first years were a real challenge. Although my salary barely covered the rent, I was determined to make it work. I never had to balance my checking account because there were only a few dollars left when I withdrew my final 20 dollars right before the next payday. But I knew how to live on a budget. I cooked a big pot of tomato sauce each Sunday for my meals throughout the week. To mix it up, I made a tray of seven-layer dip with refried beans and guacamole. With a couple of flour tortillas, I would prepare mini burritos that contained enough protein to fill me up. Each day I would choose between the two options.

By the time Jim came into my life, my finances had improved slightly. I was teaching full-time as well as maintaining my position at the Mission. But I still had to be careful with every penny I spent. Although the years leading up to Jim's advent into my life were exciting and lively, I had accrued a huge balance on my credit card. In addition to general living expenses, my Master of Music degree was financed solely by that card.

In many ways, Jim brought order to my life. By combining our incomes, we were able to live within our means and enjoy a reasonable standard of living. A few years later, Jim got a job that required weekly travel. Even though it was a significant change in our daily routine, we were thrilled with his pay increase. His raise was more than double my current salary. It propelled us into an entirely different income bracket. I can vividly picture the Christmas that followed his promotion. Because of his extensive travel schedule, we decided to purchase all our Christmas gifts from a catalog and have them delivered to our families in Connecticut and Texas. We fondly referred to that holiday as our "Tiffany Christmas"; everyone got a beautiful ornament or holiday-themed gift from Tiffany.

By the year 2000, we had acquired a collection of beautiful antiques and elegant furniture; our home was a glorious setting for a holiday party. The Christmas tree was a Douglas fir, and it stood taller than the ones we had put up in previous years. Its fuller shape provided enough strong branches to support the many ornaments we had collected over time. I love Christmas ornaments, especially those that are blown glass with an antique look. We had collected numerous hand-painted images of Santa Claus in all shapes and sizes. There's something about the illumination of the lights reflected off them that gave the tree a majestic glow. I purchased an ornament wherever I traveled, and each one held great significance for me with memories of new adventures. Since Jim's job took him all over the world, he brought back unique ornaments from Germany, Switzerland, South Africa, and many other countries.

It was Sunday afternoon, and I was busy stringing the lights, wrapping each individual branch from the trunk out to the tip. That was the way Jim had decorated the many trees of his wealthy clients in Washington, D.C. It was labor-intensive and time-consuming, but the results were magnificent. Twinkling lights gleamed deep within the tree through to the edge of each limb. They reflected their colors off each cherished ornament and made all the work well worth the effort. I wanted our tree to look like a mini version of the tree at Rockefeller Center in New York City. Jim had taught me this method of wrapping the lights on each branch, but he had long ago handed the duty over to me. He hated stringing lights more than I did. And I was the one who was determined to achieve the ideal twinkling result.

While I strung the lights, Jim pulled out the many boxes of decorations and began to unwrap each ornament and place it on the coffee table. With Christmas music playing in the background, the two of us began to lace the tree with our treasures. This was one of our significant rituals – we have always marked special moments, and they become part of our family tradition. Perhaps that is because we are both ex-seminarians and both value ritual.

I was very particular about the placement of each ornament. Those that were more beautiful or meaningful would have a place of prominence on the tree, at eye level, in the front. In order to give it balance, the bigger ornaments hung at the bottom of the tree and the smaller ones we set up higher. As usual, Jim placed one of the larger ornaments near the top. As he turned to get another, I quietly removed it and put it near the wide part of the tree. He turned and spotted me in the midst of my covert operation.

"Caught you! What's wrong with where I put that?"

"What? What do you mean?" I asked innocently.

"Should I just let you finish decorating by yourself?"

"No, no, of course not. I'm just very particular about where each one goes!"

"Tell me something I don't know."

We laughed and continued our ritual, recalling stories or memories connected to so many of the ornaments represented. No matter how busy we were, we set aside an afternoon or evening to decorate our Christmas tree each year. It marked the beginning of the season for us.

During the holiday season, our condo was a Christmas wonderland. Because I had numerous concert performances and liturgies to conduct, we made sure to put up our tree right after Thanksgiving. I loved decorating each floor of the house and hanging lights on the deck with fresh pine garland adorning every banister in our home. The tree was on the top floor, looking out towards downtown San Francisco and its reflection in the windows blended with the twinkling lights of the city skyline.

We were preparing for our annual holiday open house. The guest list of nearly 100 people included the members of the Mission Dolores Choir, work friends, and neighbors. Jim and I loved to cook and bake, so there wasn't even a passing thought about hiring a caterer; both of us spent days in the kitchen. I used recipes from my Italian mother and made loaves of homemade spinach and onion bread, fresh pasta with pesto, and baked ziti. Jim's mom had taught him to wrap the roasted turkey with cheesecloth in order to preserve the moisture. As the turkey was basted, the cheesecloth would absorb all of the juices and become golden brown. When it was fully cooked, he unwrapped the turkey and used the cheesecloth, saturated with turkey drippings, to make the most wonderful buttery gravy. There were jumbo shrimp carefully arranged in the form of a Christmas tree, giant wedges of cheese, dips, and baked ham. We made focaccia, which is a type of Italian pizza, and platters of vegetables – asparagus, green beans, and Brussels sprouts – each covered in a different sauce. The dessert table was piled high with so many of my favorites: butternut and sugar cookies, cupcakes, red velvet cake with cream cheese frosting, cheesecake, and fruit pies.

We extended the dining room table to its fullest length and, by using of boxes of multiple heights and sizes, created numerous levels where we would place the food. We covered every surface with red and green tablecloths that produced a sweeping holiday landscape. I painstakingly polished our two silver candelabras that Jim brought back from Greece. They adorned either end of the table along with pine branches and poinsettias. It was a beautiful stage on which to display all our delectable delights. Once the food was in place, it was a feast.

A few years earlier, we had acquired an exquisite antique 1890 Steinway grand piano whose sound was warm and full. With its empire legs and scrolled music stand, it stood prominently in our living room and was the main focal point as people entered our home. Behind the piano were the glass doors to our balcony, framed by a handsome set of drapes that Jim had designed and made. I had the piano tuned and made sure that there were copies of Christmas carols and sheet music from my choir's recent concert nearby.

I loved conducting the choir at Mission Dolores Basilica. Many of those talented singers were our San Francisco family and dearest of friends. It was inevitable that at some point in the evening, we would gather around the Steinway to sing choir pieces and carols in four-part harmony. When that repertoire was exhausted, we would launch into show tunes. Jim and I often hosted dinner parties to bring people together. It's what we did; that was our thing. We loved gathering different groups of people at our table, deepening friendships, and creating new ones.

That year, Jim and I designed Christmas ornaments with the image of the historic Old Mission in San Francisco. We gave one to each member of the choir and all our neighbors and friends who joined in our festivities. It was an exciting time, and it truly felt like we were on top of the world.

The party was a great success with friends dropping by throughout the afternoon and evening. Both Jim and I were in our element as we worked our way through each group – refilling the shrimp bowl, opening more wine, and washing glasses. There were people of all ages, retirees to college students, and every age in between. We had straight, gay, lesbian, single, and coupled friends representing many backgrounds and ethnicities. It was a truly diverse crowd.

CHAPTER 3

In our neighborhood, right above the Castro district, we had a whole crew of friends right nearby. Many of us had met through our four-legged family members while on our daily walks. Alex, our Dalmatian, would fly up the steep incline to Kite Hill to meet her furry friends, and I followed a good distance behind her. She would announce my arrival, and then I would enjoy some conversation with our neighbors.

The unobstructed view from the hilltop was expansive. Flanked by the two huge hills of Twin Peaks, and topped with the red and white Sutro Tower, Kite Hill looked east to Oakland and the San Francisco bay. All of the city and the Bay Bridge lay before us on those daily walks; it was one of the most beautiful vista points in the city. But when the fog rolled in during the summer months, it was blustery and cold up there. I was never without my heavy coat and scarf for those typical August afternoons.

Alex played with every dog that was willing. I used a racket to hit her tennis ball as far as I could, and she leapt to catch it on the first bounce. She looked so graceful as she caught her prize in mid-air, her muscles flexing in her sleek body. She was a beautiful Dalmatian and could have been a show dog had she not been born deaf. I joked that she was the athlete in the family because neither Jim nor I were into sports. As she got older, rather than run and jump to catch her tennis ball, she would sit on the bench beside me and sniff at the cool, foggy air.

Meanwhile, I was shivering in the wind, wishing that the sun would come out, and the fog would burn off. I longed for sunnier weather and warmer summers, "real summers" with hot, sultry nights and warm breezes. I dreamed of wearing shorts and t-shirts rather than sweatshirts and long pants in August. The summer fog would get me a bit down, and I nostalgically recalled childhood memories of life back east in Connecticut. As I reminisced, I conveniently forgot about the oppressive humidity and ever-present mosquitoes during the summer months, or the 20-degree days and brutal snowstorms of winter. I romanticized those frigid winters with images of sitting by a fireplace watching the snow gently falling. Time and distance obscured the memories of backbreaking shoveling, canceled plans, and driving in icy conditions.

I still loved San Francisco, but there were other challenges that had nothing to do with the weather. For many years, Jim's job took him all over the world to implement new database software. That included traveling to Europe, Asia, and Africa, often for two and three weeks at a time. Given the time differences in each country, it was difficult for us to have regular conversations. One of us was usually just waking up in the morning or had already gone to bed at the end of the day. This made his time away even more difficult for me, and we felt very disconnected from each other.

Upon his return, our routine included eating at Bacco, our favorite neighborhood restaurant. Though I understood that Jim would be exhausted, I enthusiastically anticipated his arrival as I sat at the airport waiting to pick him up. On our drive to the restaurant in San Francisco, I would begin my patter, trying to fill him in on all that had happened while he was away.

We would drive directly to the restaurant that was a mere 10-minute walk from home. Bacco was comprised of no more than 15 tables, so it was very intimate. The waiters were from Rome and greeted us like family each week. I would immediately strike up a conversation so that I could practice my rusty Italian. Jim and I would order our meals and chat about how much we had missed each other while he was gone. As we brought each other up to date, his jet lag would set in, and his eyes would begin to droop. My anticipation for his return and my excitement at seeing him were dampened by his exhaustion. Once we finished our entrees, there was no consideration of dessert; he had to get home and into bed. This was the routine each time he returned. He would crash in the midst of our meal and then spend a significant part of the next day recovering. So even when he was home, we spent little quality time together.

We were both elated when Jim accepted a new job in San Diego, and there was a marked improvement in our lives. Rather than being in a foreign country for weeks at a time, he was in California. Because he was now in the same time zone, we could have our nightly conversations just before heading to bed. Jim commuted to San Diego each week; he flew down on Monday mornings and returned home every Thursday evening. Although we only got four nights together each week, it was an enormous improvement over his previous travel schedule.

Jim was immersed in the high tech craze of the nineties, and he loved his job. His career sky-rocketed along with his salary, so we compensated for the time spent apart by zipping across the globe for brief vacations when time would allow. We went to Portugal for the World Expo during the summer, the Virgin Islands for a bare-boat cruise during the Christmas holidays, and New Zealand for Easter. It was all so exotic and fabulous. I had never have imagined myself experiencing the extravagant life that we were leading.

Even so, we missed spending ordinary time together. Our daily lives were largely spent apart. Jim used to sing in the Mission Dolores choir I directed, and many of us would go out for drinks after rehearsals. Jim was demonstrably involved in my professional life as well and was proud of my accomplishments. He had attended each of the many performances by my high school choirs, and I missed having him there to support me and debrief with me following the concerts. During the time spent away from home, Jim filled his evenings by working late into the night. By the time he got back home to me each Thursday, he was completely wiped out.

The commute to San Diego ended another significant ritual – our nightly dinners together. Dinnertime was always a sacred time for us. Though he was a complete workaholic who often worked late into the evenings, I always waited for him to come home so that we could eat together. I cooked our meals during the weekdays, and he'd cook on the weekends. Each night I lit the candles on the table and poured us glasses of California wine. Those nightly dinners were our time to catch up, chat about the day, and share our challenges and successes. Then we would clear the table, and Jim washed the dishes as I dried and put everything away. After cleaning up, there was little time to relax before bedtime. Even so, our nightly dinners were an essential means of re-connecting. Our time together at our table brought us back in sync at the end of the day.

While he was away, I missed that ordinary but essential ritual. Jim filled the void by working until late at night, but I wallowed in my loneliness. Rather than watch a movie I wanted to see, I would try to wait until he was home so that we could see it together. I remember seeing or hearing something interesting and thinking, "Jim would love this." I ended up spending much of my time waiting rather than living. It soon became apparent that I had to become more engaged with my friends during the weeknights. I started attending social gatherings alone and went to movies and out to dinner with friends. I was leading a life that was similar to my single days, yet I always felt that a part of me was missing. I began to feel depressed.

To combat this, I threw myself into my work to fill the emptiness. I was in my tenth year as Director of Music at Mission Dolores Basilica. The Mission is the founding building of the city of San Francisco, and tour buses parked in front of the church were a common sight. At each Sunday mass, there were tourists from around the country and the world. The choir sang rousing spirituals or chorales during the Mass, and each week we would get an enthusiastic round of applause after singing the post-communion choral piece. The applause became such a regular part of our weekly liturgies that, at one point, the pastor grew upset and asked me to stop the congregation from clapping. He was a very progressive guy so I was surprised by his admonishment. In contrast, the pastor that was assigned to the church after him loved the choir and knew that it brought many new people to Mass. In fact, he would often initiate the applause.

The Basilica choir was my main creative outlet. It consisted of approximately 50 to 60 members, many of whom were strong singers with solid musical backgrounds. The choir had recently returned from a wildly successful concert tour of southern Italy the previous summer. We toured Rome, Assisi, and further south to the Province of Bari, Calabria, and over to Sicily. One of the highlights for me was the concert in my parents' hometown of Bisceglie, Bari. The Cathedral was packed, and by the start of the concert, there was standing room only. I walked over to my music stand, and the audience greeted me like a long-lost son or celebrity. My parents and siblings had traveled with us on that tour and were treated like royalty.

The day following the concert, the mayor received the choir at city hall where he presented us with a plaque engraved with my name. There were posters hanging throughout the city with a photograph of the choir and the words, "Son of Bisceglie returns to give a concert at the Cathedral." It was a great tribute to my parents. The audience included many extended family and friends, and during the concert, they felt comfortable enough to correct my Italian each time I attempted to introduce a song, explain its meaning, or translate the lyrics. It was quite funny, and everyone was amused by my public Italian language lessons. We had huge audiences at all of our other concerts. In the town of Taormina in Sicily, people recognized me days after our performance. They stopped me in the streets to compliment the choir and me. Back home in San Francisco, our reputation grew quickly, and that year nearly a thousand people attended our annual Christmas concert.

In addition to my position at the Mission, I taught at Sacred Heart Cathedral Prep, where I was chair of the Visual and Performing Arts Department, as well as Director of Publications. I had started the music program from scratch eight years earlier, and my concert choir numbered 130 singers. I organized international concert tours each year, and in the year 2000, we traveled to Italy for a performance in celebration of the millennium. My students were great fun and always kept me on my toes. It's hard to believe that I traveled all over Europe and Asia with two full busloads of teenagers. But I have always loved working with that age group because of their incredible energy and candor. That choir was also building a reputation at home. They were the largest high school choir in the Bay area, and that year they sang for the opening and dedication of the San Francisco International Terminal.

I was always busy, and I began to feel the emotional as well as the physical strain in my body. I was having significant rotator cuff issues in my conducting arm. I started seeing an orthopedic doctor to get regular treatments of acupuncture and ultrasound. After every concert or rehearsal, I had to place an ice pack on my shoulder due to the throbbing; it burned as if it were on fire. Though I was experiencing a great deal of notoriety in San Francisco, I began to get discouraged about the lack of advancement in my musical career and felt that I was stuck in a rut. It seemed that I was never content with my accomplishments. I continually sought out something bigger and better.

My drive to reach for greater things has always been my greatest motivator and my greatest curse. And because of that, I was never fully satisfied with my current positions. My attempts to acquire other choirs or college teaching positions did not yield positive results. I sent my résumé out to each and every choral position posted in the Bay Area to no avail. San Francisco is a small city, and the number of posts for choral directors was limited. It seemed that once a director was hired, she or he would remain there for decades; there was very little turnover. I was frustrated and felt that my professional life had reached a plateau. I believed I had achieved all that I could at Mission Dolores and was interested in working beyond church-related choirs. I became restless and sought to change my life.

I longed for something more than the crazy, interminably busy schedules that we found ourselves following. During performance weeks, I began having trouble sleeping through the night. Eventually, sleepless nights became the norm for me. I would often get out of bed, go to my computer, and begin the day's work. This became a chronic problem as my anxiety mounted; I did much of my work at 4:00 in the morning. I began to find myself without my usual motivation and creativity. Even traveling became a chore; I no longer got excited about visiting new places and shopping for unusual items for our home. That alone should have been a red flag for anyone who knew me. Traveling had always been a great passion for me, and shopping in those new and exciting places was a natural consequence. As I planned my two concert tours for the following spring and summer, I felt that it was more of a burden than an adventure. There was obviously something wrong, but I couldn't name it.

CHAPTER 4

Our best friends Dan and Steve had just adopted an infant girl. Katherine was an absolute joy. Steve worked at city hall, just a few blocks from my school. I picked up Katherine at daycare after school several days a week and brought her home until one of them would come by to pick her up after work. She and I had a special bond from those months together. But even though I was only taking care of her for three hours a day, I felt the strain.

One of the craziest moments with Katherine will be imprinted in my memory forever. I had just brought her into the condo and climbed up to the third floor. Alex, our Dalmatian, loved Katherine. Perhaps that's because babies always have some sort of food on their hands and fingers. By that time, Katherine was walking well, so I had to keep my eyes on her at all times. It was especially significant near the stairs going down to the next level of the house.

She was running around giggling because Alex was trying to lick her when I noticed a dark spot running up her back. She had had an explosion; it was everywhere, down her legs and around her belly. Katherine didn't seem to mind at all; she was having a great time running away from me while Alex was in hot pursuit. I got nervous as she got close to the stairs. I finally got a hold of her and tried to get her cleaned up as I battled to keep Alex from sneaking in to sniff her. It was disgusting, and I couldn't quite figure out how to get her clean. I did the best I could, using up all of the baby wipes, but it was still all over her. When I recounted the story to Dan later that evening, he burst out laughing.

"Why didn't you just get into the shower with her? You could have rinsed her right off."

"You know, Dan, it never occurred to me. That would have been so much easier."

My bond with Katherine was incredibly significant to

me–my heart was bursting when we spent those afternoons alone. I was privileged enough to take care of her during her first year of life. Her explosion notwithstanding, I truly enjoyed our time together. That little vignette, however, gave me a tiny glimpse into how difficult it is to be a parent.

I assumed that my emotional state was similar to most of our other overworked friends, and perhaps it was. Dan and Steve's lives were quite full. Their demanding jobs, along with the responsibilities of caring for a newborn baby, made it even more challenging. They found that their lives were much too busy and hectic; we all believed that we had lost balance. Each of us spent much more time and energy on work than at home with each other. We rushed from one appointment or event to the next. This was the topic of many conversations, and we were all frustrated. There was no time to simply rest and relax.

During that time, I was working seven days a week, and I realized that I needed to divest of one of my positions. It was a tough decision for me. After teaching full-time during the week, I found that it was exhausting to work at the Mission every weekend, especially considering that Jim was only home during that time. The choir members were like family to me, and the music we made together created some of the most fulfilling musical experiences I had ever

had. I couldn't imagine giving that up, but I had to let go
of something – my emotional and physical health were
suffering.

The struggle to let go of either job weighed heavily
upon me. I truly loved each position that I held. My work
at the high school gave me a musical as well as a creative
intellectual outlet. Through the desktop publishing,
photography, and editing of the school's quarterly magazine,
I was able to use a very different skill set. On the other side
of the equation, Mission Dolores fulfilled so many of my
musical needs because the choir included a number of adults
who were fine musicians. I was able to challenge myself and
the choir with the challenging repertoire that I programmed.
In addition, those men and women were a central social
circle for both Jim and me. Some of our closest friends were
from the parish, and I couldn't imagine leaving that part of
my life behind. But as Director of Music at the Basilica, I
had to work every weekend and all major Church holidays.
Because of that, I would start the workweek exhausted from
the weekend. It was challenging to plan a weekend getaway
when Jim was home.

It seemed that giving up my work at Mission Dolores
was the most logical decision I could make. To compensate
for that loss, I thought that I could start a community choir

comprised of the members of the Basilica Choir along with recent graduates from the high school. I hoped that might fulfill my musical need, keep my rapport with friends that I had come to love and care for while eliminating working on weekends and holidays. It seemed to be the best solution. Although I was still teaching full-time, I would no longer have to work each weekend.

After ten successful and joyous years at Mission Dolores, I submitted my resignation. I had accomplished a great deal during my years as director. The choir had grown from 12 or so members to 60, and it was well regarded throughout the bay area. My last day and final performance would be our Christmas concert.

My parents surprised me and flew in from Connecticut to attend the final concert. The atmosphere was electric; the energy was festive, and the choir, orchestra, and audience were all having fun. The church was at capacity, and the choir was at its best; it was an excellent performance. For the encore, I asked that anyone who had ever sung in one of my choirs come up to sing. I promised that they would all know the song. The South African anti-Apartheid song, "Freedom is Coming," had become an anthem for each of my choirs. I could not think of a song more appropriate to mark the new chapter in our lives.

As the audience members flowed onto the stage, I could hardly believe my eyes. There were hundreds of singers in the sanctuary, including young people, retired people, and singers who had gone on to start families or had moved away. My high school students who were in attendance joined the choir as well. I was flooded with great emotion and pride. As I cued each voice, the sound grew stronger and more vibrant. Soon the Basilica was filled with this great anthem for freedom and justice. I felt that I was floating upon the melody, and each singer was woven into my life through the lush harmonies that were being voiced by that great choir.

It is truly one of the highlights of my life. I was touching something much more significant than any individual singer. I was touching the face of the divine, and I felt it tingling throughout my entire being as all that creative energy was channeled through me. I was as happy as I have ever been. My choir and the parishioners gave me a great send-off with a grand reception following the concert. I was presented with a hand-painted page from a medieval songbook, and the frame was inscribed with my name and the dates of my tenure as music director. It was a beautiful tribute to my time as director of music at Mission Dolores.

CHAPTER 5

Jim and I planned a vacation to celebrate my newfound freedom. When the high school let out for Christmas break, we were going to fly to the Caribbean for a week of sailing. We had a boat in California for five years and were able to sail her year-round. Jim had taught me to sail on the San Francisco Bay; it proved to be more than a little challenging due to the high wind gusts and quickly changing weather conditions. But I learned to love it and enjoyed the thrill of the heeling sailboat in high winds as it cut through the waves.

The previous year, we had boarded our boat for a New

Year's Eve sail. I was at the helm as we neared the Bay Bridge. The winds were around 20 knots with 30-knot gusts, which is the norm on the bay, but the night was clear. The lights of the cityscape twinkled as we sailed right by the Transamerica building, and I caught the wind at just the right angle. The sailboat heeled so far to one side that I had to brace my foot on the seat of the port side to keep balanced. It was then that I heard the familiar warning, "Mario..." I knew that Jim wanted me to back off a bit and straighten the boat. I reluctantly followed his advice. I loved the feeling of the wind in the sails and the sound of the boat cutting through the waves at such speed.

After an energetic sail under the Bay Bridge, we anchored off Treasure Island to ring in the new millennium. We cooked a gourmet dinner for several friends, and then gathered up on deck to pop the cork of a bottle of champagne and filled our commemorative flutes that were etched with the year 2000. When midnight arrived, we toasted to our good fortune and marveled at the spectacular display of fireworks against the San Francisco skyline.

Given the weather patterns in the Bay Area, I had never sailed in warm or calm weather. While planning the itinerary for our Caribbean trip, Jim colorfully recounted his memories of sailing on the Chesapeake Bay when he was living in Washington, D.C. There were tales of leisurely sails and warm breezes while sipping wine. This was utterly foreign to my experience of sailing on the chilly San Francisco Bay. Jim promised that I would fall in love with sailing all over again. With warm, steady breezes and calmer waters, sailing in the Virgin Islands would be an entirely different experience.

The weeks before our departure date, I made several visits to a tanning salon in order to get a base tan so that I wouldn't burn to a crisp once we got there. I was so looking forward to our trip; when the day arrived, I could hardly contain my excitement. We had an overnight stop in Puerto Rico and arrived on December 23 amid all the festive celebrations on the island. It was the first time that I was not working on Christmas Eve and Christmas Day in more than ten years. I could hardly believe that we were in San Juan and that I wasn't stressed out about all of the services I had to direct.

We wandered the quaint streets of Old San Juan, where the influences of Spain were all around us. The architecture and the island's history as a territory of Spain made me feel as if I were in Europe rather than the Caribbean.

The palm trees were wrapped in little twinkling lights, colors jumped out at us from every direction, and music filled the air. The smells of fresh seafood and garlic surrounded us and whetted our appetites. We decided to stop at a restaurant with outdoor seating. I ordered ceviche for the first time and a tall tropical drink. We both felt free for the first time in years. After dinner, we strolled down the avenue and listened to the excitement of the holiday festivities. Christmas music of all sorts floated out of each bar and could be heard on every street corner; the atmosphere was vibrant and exotic.

The following day we flew to St. Thomas to take possession of the boat for the week. During the short ride from the airport, we marveled at the abundance of natural beauty all around us. With white-sand beaches and clear, cerulean water, it was a feast of the eyes. We made our way to the Marina and registered at the office. I was anxious to see the sailboat so, while Jim filled out the paperwork, I wandered the docks trying to imagine which boat was ours. We had rented a 43-foot sailboat that we would captain ourselves. She was a significantly larger boat than our 38-foot boat back in San Francisco, and it was going to be great fun to sail her. The galley was much more spacious, and the sleeping cabins were huge. Since we were there first, we lay claim to the captain's cabin because it had a bathroom in it. It was a bit self-serving, but we knew our friends wouldn't care. Since we arrived the day before our sailing buddies, Mark and Cheryl, we went to the local grocery stores and stocked the boat with food and drink.

It was December 24, 2000, Christmas Eve in St. Thomas. Instead of fir trees, there were tall, wispy palm trees everywhere wrapped in white lights and lining the waterfront and main streets. The warm breezes grazed our cheeks, and the sound of the water lapping against the hull of the boat invited us to rest for the first time in a long while.

That night, we had Christmas dinner at a small restaurant that was a short walk from the Marina. A local couple that loved fine dining and good wine owned it. The menu at Sally's was French with a Caribbean flair. It was an incredibly romantic dinner. Jim and I selected a robust cabernet from their extensive wine list, and we reveled in our escape from the insanity of our busy lives. The dinner was as elegant a meal as we had had in our favorite San Francisco restaurants. The dessert was scrumptious, and the wine was excellent, especially given that we were California wine snobs. We sat back in our food and wine haze and took it all in. We were thousands of miles away from home on a

Caribbean island. No one could get in touch with us because there was sparse cell service there.

The rest of the week turned out to be just as magical. That night I used a pay telephone to place a call to Bill and Debbie, two of our dear friends in San Francisco. They had just sung for midnight mass at Mission Dolores. I felt a sweet sadness. I loved that service, and my heart ached to be with our friends in the choir. They filled me in on how it all went.

"The usual crew was there, and we sang our bi-lingual Christmas music, but it just wasn't the same. We really missed you, Mario."

"Yeah, it felt odd not to be there. I miss you guys too."

I was a bit melancholy after I hung up as the reality of my resignation from the Mission set in. I knew that I was going to miss it terribly, and I began to question my decision to leave my post. What was I thinking? I love that choir. But, as I looked at the gently swaying palm trees dressed in their Christmas best, I wasn't sad for long. I was confident that I had made the right decision because I needed to simplify my life. It was time to start taking better care of myself.

The next day when Mark and Cheryl joined us on the sailboat Pleiades, we set sail to each of the other U.S.

Virgin Islands as well as the B.V.I. We snorkeled when we felt the urge, dropped anchor where the beauty of the shore called to us, and toasted to each sunset. My aversion to cold foods meant that I was cooking each meal unless we decided to go to shore and dine. Since I like to eat, I had every menu planned out: quesadillas with guacamole, penne all'arrabbiata, and vodka sauce, among others. Needless to say, we did not go hungry.

Anchored off of Tortola, B.V.I., we found that a school of nurse sharks was circling the boat. I counted eight to ten of them, and they varied in size from three to 10 feet in length. They are harmless, but I didn't know that at the time. After tossing them some of our lunch, I discovered that they liked bread and cold cuts. Jim pulled out our video camera and got some great footage. Soon I had them eating out of my hands. Perched on the stern of the boat, I was leaning out to feed them while holding on to the grab-handle beside the ladder. I had let go in order to reach a shark that was a bit further out when I lost my balance. I reached back to get hold of the handle but instead grabbed the extendable ladder. It released into the water, and I plunged into the midst of the circling sharks. The ladder hit my head. Although it was nothing serious, I began to bleed. I thrashed about in the water so frantically that I am sure I didn't even get wet. Thankfully, my graceful dive into the water immediately scared off the sharks that were much more startled than I was. When I regained my composure, I looked up to see Jim, Mark, and Cheryl laughing hysterically on the deck. Clearly, they knew that I was not in any danger. With my pride wounded, I swam back and boarded the boat. To add to my shame, Jim had filmed the entire episode. That was the last time I fed sharks with our leftover lunch.

After a week of bathing suits and tee shirts, we dressed up for the first time for a special New Year's Eve dinner. The four of us hopped onto the eight-foot dinghy and motored across the waterfront in St. Thomas with only a few minor splashes to wet us. We had an idyllic dinner at the restaurant at Blackbeard's Castle, which sat perched upon a hill looking over the beautiful harbor. Afterward, we sat beside the pool, gazing at the stars above us. I had never witnessed such brilliance in the night sky; there were hundreds of thousands of stars sparkling above us. We were each lost in our thoughts and reveled at the beauty of the heavens above. We were content to be with each other and to ring in the New Year in our own quiet yet festive way. That was when I began to dream about returning to the Caribbean to make a life there for Jim and me. I turned to Jim, and I said, "Let's just send for our stuff."

He laughed and responded, "Hmm, I don't know who you think we are, but I'm pretty sure we don't have people to do that for us! But it is wonderful here on the islands."

"Yeah, I could get used to this," I said dreamily.

And so our fantasy of life in the Caribbean began.

CHAPTER 6

My routine changed dramatically once we returned to San Francisco. It felt luxurious to be sleeping late on the weekends and having Sundays free. Jim made scones and prepared lavish breakfasts every weekend, while I quietly sipped my coffee and looked out over the city skyline. He and I reminisced about our perfect week in the Caribbean, and I was determined to re-capture our experience in St. Thomas. Unbeknownst to Jim, I began to investigate the laws regarding employment in the Virgin Islands and discovered that no work visas were necessary since it was a U.S. territory. I then scoured the real estate sites for homes on St. Thomas and St. John. Much to my delight, the houses were hundreds of thousands of dollars less than in San Francisco. That meant that if we were to move there, we could buy a sailboat as well as a house. I knew that Jim wouldn't be able to resist the idea of launching our Caribbean life with a new sailboat. Rather than gather people in our home in San Francisco, we would do so on our 50-foot yacht!

Jim tried to persuade me to slow down, to really think about what we would be leaving behind. He has always been the voice of reason and practicality, a quality that I have needed in my life. I always dove in head-first and dealt with the repercussions of my decisions afterward. He says that I place myself in the path of an oncoming train; after it hits, I pick up the pieces. There were always unexpected consequences for my adventures. His reasonable argument caused me to pause. He pointed to my successful choirs and the joy I received from working with my young students.

"Look at what you've built at the high school. They didn't even have a choir when you started there! How could you leave that behind?"

"I do love them, but I'm getting bored, Jim. Doesn't life in the Caribbean sound fabulous?"

"And what about the choir at Mission Dolores? You

love those people. What about Dan and Steve, and little Katherine? You would really miss them," Jim argued.

"Yeah, I would miss them," I said. "But we'll visit, and I am sure our friends will all want to take trips to the Caribbean to see us. Who wouldn't want a free place to stay on an island paradise?"

He tried to get me to see that our lives in San Francisco were full and beautiful. He tried to make me realize that our San Francisco family would be difficult to leave, but I couldn't see beyond my excitement for a new life. I was looking for an escape from all the stress. Looking back on it, I can see that I was in the midst of a worsening anxiety condition. All I wanted to do was run away from it all. His reasonable arguments fell on deaf ears, and I continued my manic search for the ideal life in the islands.

Talking about buying a 50-foot sailboat was like dangling a carrot in front of a horse. There was just so much resistance that Jim could muster. The prospect of giving up our jobs to sail the Caribbean was much too enticing, especially when this plan would mean early retirement for both of us.

The wheels were set in motion, and the momentum was unstoppable. Or rather, I was unstoppable. I'm sure that

Jim believed I would simply lose steam and forget about my crazy idea, but it just got more intense. I made contact with a realtor in St. Thomas, who would later become a dear friend. I compiled a list of properties that were in our price range and asked her to check on them. She sent me links to a number of properties and described where they were on the island and what issues each one had. It was interesting to learn that there were hardly any beachfront properties. The volcanic nature of the Virgin Islands provided dramatic hills and cliffs looking out over the water, but few beaches upon which to build a home. In addition, we learned that all beaches were public. One issue that concerned me was the number of hurricanes that had ripped through the islands in recent years. I wanted to make sure that we were in a protected part of the island, assuming there was such a place.

After a few months of searching, I convinced Jim to go to St. Thomas to see some of the properties that were available. I could not take any time away from school, as we were preparing for our spring concert tour. Our realtor had a small apartment below her home where Jim could stay during his short visit. So, with his video camera in hand, he visited each of the houses I had found as well as others that the realtor recommended.

Upon his return, he played the footage and shared his thoughts on each property. One was perched directly on the edge of the water, and you could hear the surf crashing on the rocks below. It was the most dramatic of the houses he visited, but the road leading to it was not paved and was filled with huge potholes and rocks. It took nearly 25 minutes to get to the house after turning off the main road. Another had beautiful views with an expansive deck that surrounded the house, but it was built entirely of wood – the fire insurance would be exorbitant. But there was one beautiful home nestled against a hillside with a beautiful view of Magens Bay. It was terra-cotta colored with cobalt blue shutters and white trim. It had an extensive veranda that spanned the entire length of the house, and both of us loved it.

When I asked Jim what it was like on the island and whether he could picture us there, he said,

"Mario, the shoreline is absolutely gorgeous, and you've seen how beautiful the water is. But there's a great deal of poverty there. There are homes that were destroyed in the last hurricane and never rebuilt. The wreckage of those houses dots the entire island. There are people living in corrugated metal shacks and chickens roaming around the garbage dumpsters that are in every neighborhood. It's not all as beautiful and glamorous as you might want to believe. I think it would be a difficult adjustment for us."

"But the house is beautiful, right? Can you picture us living there?"

"I'm not sure, Mario. In many ways, it's very primitive."

"Did you go to the marinas to ask about renting a slip for a boat? That would certainly feel luxurious."

"Let's just say that the islands look better from the water."

I desperately wanted Jim to tell me that it would be perfect for us in St. Thomas. We continued to discuss whether the good outweighed the bad. I didn't absorb any of the information regarding the difficulty of life on the islands. I was determined that it would all work out, and after a few weeks, our excitement won out. We decided to make an offer on our favorite house. But by the time we decided to act, there was already an accepted contract on it. We took that as a sign to slow down and let the prospect of moving rest for a while. That wasn't hard to do since I was in the midst of concert preparations, and our lives in San Francisco continued to spin. Even without having to work each weekend at the Mission, my schedule continued to keep me running. It was easy enough to forget about my island dream while planning a European concert tour for the high school in April and a summer tour for the community choir I had just founded. Over time, I was able to fill the empty spaces in my schedule with more activities and events.

About a month had passed when we got a call from our realtor down in St. Thomas. The deal on "our" house had fallen through, and she asked if we would still like to put an offer on it. So much for the sign telling us to slow down. Jim was working in San Diego, so our discussions were all by phone. We talked about it briefly, figured that we had little to lose, and decided to make an offer. To our surprise, it was accepted almost immediately.

From then on, everything seemed to be in "fast-forward." We put our condo on the market and received multiple offers; it sold for well over the asking price. We were thrilled because we were then able to purchase the house in St. Thomas as well as a 50-foot sailboat. Our dream was to charter sailing adventures down the chain of islands in the Caribbean.

Shopping for sailboats was great fun. We went to a number of boat shows and marinas in the Bay Area and boarded many different brands of sailboats. Some were more suited to racing, others for ocean voyages, still others for casual sailing. The boat we settled on was beautiful. The captain's cabin had a queen-size bed and a large bathroom in it with a separate shower. The upholstery was deep blue leather, and the galley was huge with two refrigerators and a freezer. There were two other sleeping cabins that would be perfect for guests.

Rather than have it delivered to St. Thomas, Jim convinced me that sailing it there would be an adventure not to be missed. We could take delivery of it on the East Coast and sail it down to the Virgin Islands ourselves. It was very tempting, so I reluctantly agreed. I have never been a big fan of sailing in the open ocean, but this was just one of many new experiences that awaited us.

I was more than a little nostalgic when our belongings were packed up and loaded on a shipping container heading for the islands. It was going to take six to seven weeks for it to arrive at its destination. Dan and Steve agreed to let us stay with them during the month of August because we had to get out of our condo. It was during that time that I began to question the entire plan. We no longer had a home of our own or jobs in San Francisco. Our beautiful condo was sold. It had been our anchor for the previous 13 years, and now it was gone; we both felt displaced. The excitement of the move started waning, and the reality of leaving all the friends who had become family hit both of us hard. When the school year began, I visited the campus and took some great photos of the students. So many of them could not understand why I wasn't returning to conduct the choir and felt that I had abandoned them. My heart ached as I spoke with them, and once again, I questioned my decision to leave.

The month at Dan and Steve's house seemed to pass very slowly. The only bright aspect of our stay was that we got to spend time with Katherine. The bonding that we experienced during those weeks continues to keep us close so many years later. They were so generous with us, and we were each feeling the sadness of our impending departure.

Our plan was to drive cross-country to Connecticut and spend a little time with my family before our flight to St. Thomas. We packed up our S.U.V. with boxes but kept a comfortable spot for our Dalmatian's bed. That morning we got up at 5:00 a.m., had a quick breakfast, and said our goodbyes to Dan and Steve. Since they were planning to visit us for New Year's Eve, it made the departure a bit less sad. But the heartwrenching goodbye was yet to come. I quietly opened the door to Katherine's bedroom and made my way over to her crib. I looked at her angelic face as she peacefully slept and kissed her on the forehead. I wondered if she would even remember me in four months and if we would ever be as close again as we were that day. That goodbye broke my heart.

CHAPTER
7

We got on the road before rush hour so that we wouldn't waste time in traffic. We crossed the Bay Bridge with no problem and continued on Interstate 80 for several hours. Before we knew it, we crossed over the state line into Nevada. It became clear that we had left our former lives behind. Our new adventure was ahead of us, and we began to feel our excitement return. It was a beautiful drive, and we marveled at the vast countryside of the west. The Rocky Mountains were majestic, and the national parks were marvels to see. Despite the beauty that surrounded us, we were anxious to get to Connecticut. I longed for a visit with my family before our flight down to St. Thomas. With that in mind, we decided to get in as much mileage as possible each day; that meant we were on the road for 12-14 hours.

The long days of driving didn't keep us from enjoying our time together as we tried to imagine what our lives would be like in the Caribbean. This was not uncommon for us. Jim and I enjoyed new projects, and this was to be our third house together; each one was a fixer-upper. In each case, we would picture our new home and try to imagine each room with its newly renovated decor. Designs changed or morphed into entirely different concepts as our imaginations expanded. We spent hours chatting, and our creative banter glowed with optimism. It was September of 2001, and we were ripe with the anticipation of our new lives and the exciting journey ahead of us.

Shortly after we arrived at my parents' home in Connecticut, Jim had to fly back for work in San Diego. Though this was unexpected, we welcomed the extra income. The expenses of our move to St. Thomas were mounting. He planned to return the following week for our flight on September 15. I didn't mind at all because I was busy visiting old friends and spending time with my brother and sisters. Alex, our Dalmatian, seemed to love the new surroundings, and we had a great deal of fun just hanging out. No one could quite believe that we just quit our jobs, sold everything, and were moving to an island in the Caribbean. I know that many of our friends thought we were crazy, but I believed that there might have been a bit of envy mingled in as well.

Early Tuesday morning, on September 11, I walked to the public library in town to use the Internet. Mom and Dad didn't own a computer, and I was desperate to get online. It was a crisp, bright morning; the sun was shining, and fall was in the air. I sat at the computer terminal to send a number of emails to friends, letting them know of our plans to live in the Caribbean. I read a few articles online and made my way back home.

I found my parents glued to the television; a plane had just hit one of the twin towers in New York City. We were all in shock, hungry for more information regarding the cause of the accident when, moments later, we saw the other plane hit the second tower. Nothing would be the same after that. We had cousins and friends who worked in the towers, and the worry was just beginning to mount. By that evening, we heard from my aunt that both cousins had survived, and we breathed a sigh of relief. However, our national nightmare had only just begun.

Jim was stranded in San Diego since all the airports in the country were shut down. It would be days before he could get home, and he knew that he would not be allowed to fly into JFK in New York. People were stranded all over the country with no definite word as to when they would be able to fly to their ultimate destinations. Needless to say, our plans to fly to St. Thomas that week were put on hold. We weren't even sure if we would make it there before the shipping container with all our furniture and clothes arrived. In addition, neither of us was feeling good about leaving the United States. We thought that we needed to be home, wherever that may have been. The uncertainty and the grief that the country was experiencing heightened our desire to stay.

We were finally able to fly to St. Thomas from Hartford, Connecticut, on September 17. Unfortunately, we had to change planes in San Juan. This made it very difficult for the dog. We had to give her a sedative because she would be traveling in the cargo hold. When we landed in Puerto Rico, I watched as they transferred her crate to our connecting flight to St. Thomas. She was overheated and shaking with fear; I was terribly worried about her. To make matters worse, our flight in Hartford was late, so we missed our connecting flight. The delay resulted in more time for Alex to remain alone in the extreme heat.

When we finally landed in St. Thomas, we were exhausted and stressed. I ran as quickly as I could to the baggage claim area so that I could get to Alex. To my great relief, her crate was brought in promptly. As soon as she saw me, she became more alert and pressed her nose against the metal bars of the crate; we both knew it was going to be all right. Alex was still so drugged that she could barely stand when I let her out of the crate, but her tail wagged a bit as she collapsed onto my lap, content to be reunited. That would have been a very tender moment had it not been 95 degrees with 90 percent humidity. Alex had never been in such extreme heat because her entire life was spent in the cold and foggy climate of San Francisco. We knew she had quite a challenge ahead of her. But as long as she was with her Dads, she was content. We took a taxi to the car rental company right near the airport and rented a bright yellow jeep. We immediately put the top down, hopped in, and made our way to the opposite side of the island to our realtor's rental apartment. We planned to stay there until the moving van brought our things the following Monday.

I was anxious to see our house. I had only seen photos

and the video that Jim had taken months before. So after we got settled, we immediately headed out to our new home. I could hardly contain my excitement as we drove up the driveway. There were huge arched double doors that opened into the great room with soaring cathedral ceiling. Turning towards an arched hallway, we were greeted with spectacular views of the Caribbean Sea. We had brought a cold bottle of champagne and two glasses with us. We walked out to the lanai overlooking Magens Bay and toasted to our new lives. I couldn't wait until moving day.

CHAPTER 8

The next day, we were busy with numerous tasks in preparation for the movers. Our house had been empty for some time, and the spiders and lizards had made themselves at home. There were dark lumps dripping down the walls that turned out to be gecko poop. I later discovered that mosquitoes were a significant part of their diet and was comforted by the fact that there were many fewer mosquitoes in our house to feast upon us. Cobwebs graced every corner and door lintel, and the terra-cotta floor tiles were covered with a sticky film of dirt and pollen. Armed with cleaning supplies, we got to work scouring the floors and walls.

Among the many practical details to tend to was getting a car. Jim and I were waging a campaign to simplify our lives. Leaving our jobs behind in San Francisco as well as our many commitments, we believed that we would get back in tune with what was important in life. With that in mind, we went searching for a new car that was a good fit for our island life. Originally we had thought that we would buy a jeep similar to the one we had rented. But after only a day of driving it on the island, it was clear that our backs would not be able to withstand the constant bouncing around that the jeep put us through. The roads in St. Thomas were riddled with potholes, and we were jostled, jiggled, and thrown out of our seats with every bump and hole in the road. The turnoff from the main road to our street had an unusually large hole that had to be navigated before we could get to our house. It didn't take long for us to eliminate the jeep from consideration.

There weren't many car dealerships on the island, but it didn't matter much to either of us. We just needed an inexpensive vehicle that was high enough off the ground not to get stuck in the countless potholes. We figured that a small SUV would work well.

Jim and I have a history of buying cars on lunch

breaks or particularly dull afternoons. One day, while still in San Francisco, we were having lunch in the mission district when a bright yellow Volkswagen Beetle drove by. It was the first remake of the classic car. Jim had owned one during his teen years and was curious about the new model. We drove a few blocks to the dealership to take a look at one and took it for a spin. It was an enjoyable drive, but we were shocked at the price tag. They were almost as expensive as more luxurious cars, so we went next door to the Audi dealership just to make a price comparison. Of course, we had to test-drive an Audi Q 5 while we were there. It was beautiful and had so many more amenities than the Volkswagen.

At that point, both Jim and I were getting into the idea of buying a new car. When we get into one of our buying moods, each of us eggs on the other. So Jim said,

"For this amount of money, why would anyone settle for an Audi? There's a Mercedes dealership directly beside my office. Let's just go look at them…just for fun," he added after a pause.

"We might as well. I have no idea what they cost, but that sounds fun. Let's go!!

In my mind, owning a Mercedes was simply a fantasy. That's what wealthy people drove, and we were far from rich. But I enjoyed our little adventures, so I went along with the idea. I never dreamed that we would pull the trigger and buy one.

Once at the Mercedes Benz dealership, we were immediately taken with the retro styling of the E 350. The test drive put Jim over the edge, and I knew that there would be little to hold him back. He insisted that I take over and give it a try.

"You're going to love it, Mario. It drives like no other car we've tried."

"Yeah, I'll take your word for it."

"No, seriously, you have to drive it. You're going to love it."

In truth, I was too nervous about driving such an expensive car, but I couldn't say that in front of the salesman. I didn't want to make a big deal of it, so I got into the driver's seat and put the car into gear. It was like floating on air; I felt none of the bumps in the road, and the acceleration felt like a rocket compared to my Saturn. Later that afternoon, we drove off of the lot with our beautiful black Mercedes Benz as if it was the most natural thing in the world. Our friends would often joke about our dangerous lunchtime purchases.

Even though we were in St. Thomas, we expected that the purchase could be taken care of that Saturday afternoon. It was to be our first lesson with regard to the slower pace of island life. It would be days before all the necessary paperwork was completed and we could drive our new car. There was a Suzuki dealership across from the major grocery store, so we ambled over and checked out their inventory. They had a small SUV called the Vitara, and we found one that we liked in our minimalist price range. As far as options were concerned, we wanted the bare minimum; the only non-negotiable item was air-conditioning. We took the car for a test drive in the neighborhood and were happy enough with our choice. We both felt that it was a good first step toward simplifying our lives.

When we finally picked up the car, we were both relieved to be out of the jeep. We spent the day taking care of endless chores. I was taken aback when we discovered that the island post office did not deliver mail directly to people's houses. How could this be? We were still in a United States territory. Why wouldn't the government work the same way as it did on the mainland? This was yet another lesson in island living. We drove along the waterfront to the only post office we knew of and signed up for our P.O. box. We were told to pick up larger parcels at the main window. That meant that I would have to wait in very long lines, and I wasn't happy about that either. At the time, I didn't realize that this would become a highlight of my day in the months to come. There is just so much reading and painting I could do during those days alone, and a trip to the post office was a perfect diversion.

We drove all over the island attending to our many errands, up one hill, and down another while dodging potholes and mini landslides of stone on the roads. St. Thomas and St. John were both formed by volcanic activity. As a result, the islands are incredibly hilly with steep inclines and rough terrain. None of the streets had street signs, so it was difficult to follow the directions we were given.

"Go down the road until you round that curve. Once you see the big mahogany tree, turn right. If you pass the cow, you've gone too far."

This is no exaggeration; this was the nature of the directions we were given. I still know where that particular mahogany tree takes us.

At the end of a long day, we left the level roadways of downtown Charlotte Amalie and headed up the steep hill towards Skyline Drive. The panoramic view at the crest of the island was spectacular; we could see the expansive harbor and historic buildings of Charlotte Amalie along with the cruise ships steaming away from St. Thomas for other Caribbean islands. The azure waters of the port glittered in the afternoon sun as the heat of the day began to wane. However, getting home in our new SUV proved to be somewhat challenging. We continued up the incline and had to downshift to second gear in order to keep the car from stalling. We could only drive about 15 miles per hour, and the line of cars behind us became increasingly impatient. It was a far cry from the Mercedes Benz we had just sold in San Francisco.

Once we crested the hill, we began our descent down Magens Bay Road toward our house. We planned to drop off all our purchases and take an inventory of things that we needed to do before the movers arrived later in the week. After we rounded a curve, we came upon our street and took a right turn up another steep hill. Back in second gear and without a line of cars behind us, we patiently crawled our way to our house. We turned into our driveway, and the car stalled due to the steep incline. We let the car roll down onto the street and made another attempt with the same result.

"I have an idea," said Jim. "Maybe if we get a running start, we might have enough power to get all the way up the driveway."

"It's worth a try. Go for it," I responded.

We rolled down the street for about 30 feet and put the car in gear. Jim revved the engine and began to pick up speed. When we reached the driveway, he didn't break. Instead, he took the turn at full speed and was able to get to the top of the driveway before the car lost steam. We looked at each other in disbelief.

"Jim, we can't do this every time we come home. This is just crazy."

"Yeah I know. Let's just give it a few more days. Maybe we just have to get used to driving on the island."

"I doubt that. The hills aren't going away, and unless the engine gets a miraculous upgrade, we're out of luck with this car," I argued.

Our new Vitara could barely get up our own driveway, let alone the many hills throughout the island. We had to rectify our situation before it was too late.

A few days later, we were still firm in our resolve as we returned to the dealership. I was annoyed and asked them why they didn't bring us to any of the nearby hills during our test drive. They tried to placate me and explained that the next model up, the Grand Vitara, was much better on the hills. We took one on a test drive but insisted that they take us to the steepest incline in the neighborhood. Though it wasn't great, the new car was far better on the hills. Our salesman explained that we obviously couldn't merely return one car for the other. Our three-day-old Vitara had depreciated significantly, but the dealer assured us that he would give us the best price possible on the new car. Jim and I exchanged looks. How many times have we heard that before? We were exasperated but decided to do whatever we needed to get out of the Vitara. We made the exchange, signed all the new paperwork, and were able to drive off the lot that very day with our second new car.

The new SUV looked exactly the same, but its more powerful engine was able to climb up to Skyline Drive without any issues. However, the real test was yet to come. Once on our street, we drove at a reasonable speed and made the turn into our driveway. Without any hesitation, the car was able to navigate the steep incline to the top. We cheered and patted the dashboard. After that, we named her "Grand Viagra."

CHAPTER 9

After much anticipation, moving day finally arrived, and there was a frenzy of activity in our new house. We had made sure to label each box as we packed so, as they were brought in the house, I was able to direct them to the designated rooms. Fearing that it might have been damaged in transit, I was most anxious for them to unload and set up the piano. It was packed in a crate built of wooden slats and weighed nearly 800 pounds. The movers had trouble getting it off the truck and into the house. At one point, they lost their grip, and it almost hit the ground. My heart was in my mouth, and I was sure the piano would end up smashed into pieces. Once they unloaded it and got it into place, they had no idea how to set it up. Jim and I instructed them with each step on how to affix each leg and the pedals. Luckily, it suffered only minor damage in the move. I breathed a huge sigh of relief.

The next room to be set up was our bedroom; it was huge and had a spacious master bathroom and walk-in closet. We set up the bed under the ceiling fan and put away our clothes. We diligently worked throughout the day to put as much of the house together as we could. Having been displaced for more than two months, we were anxious for it to feel like home as soon as possible. We collapsed onto the chairs on the lanai at nightfall and stared out at the view, grateful that we had gotten so much done in one day. With a cold glass of wine in our hands, we toasted. Jim clinked his glass against mine and said, "To our new island paradise."

"To our new lives away from the stresses of the city!" I responded.

Our first night in our new bedroom was interesting. The weather in September was much hotter than we had experienced on our vacation the previous Christmas. Back then, the steady breeze on the water kept us cool and refreshed. Though our bed was directly under the ceiling fan, there was little relief from the stagnant, humid air. But we were exhausted and happy to sleep in our own bed after a hard day of unpacking. As we began to drift off to sleep, an entirely unfamiliar set of sounds joined in a symphony of tropical creatures. Then out of that symphony, a bold roar of a soloist broke through, followed by another and another. It was all at once loud, high-pitched, and low-pitched with an interminable echo.

"What the hell is that?" Jim exclaimed.

"It sounds huge. What kind of animals do they have here?" I wondered.

"Maybe it's a California brown bear," Jim joked.

"Bwaaaahaha! What? Did we bring one down with us?" I chimed in.

"Where is that coming from? It sounds like they are here in our room."

"Ok, Jim, this is just creepy."

It turned out to be a family of local frogs whose call is constant at night. They were living in the cistern that was directly under our bedroom, a sizeable cavernous cell comprised of cinderblock and cement. Combined with the gallons of water that filled it, the effect amplified the song of our amphibious friends. Though the frogs were only two inches long, their calls bounced and echoed in the vast concrete megaphone, making them sound huge. We never figured out the source of those calls on that first night, or where they were coming from. We certainly never considered that they could be croaking frogs.

A bit later, the mosquitoes began to sense our presence. The bedsheet was neatly folded at the bottom of our bed, and our limbs were splayed across every inch of the mattress to catch the limited breeze provided by the ceiling fan. Then it began—that familiar, high-pitched whine circling our heads. The buzzing became louder and louder as it inched closer to our ears. I batted at it and slapped my ears only to have it return to whisper its poisonous song into my ear again. It was torture. Jim couldn't stand it and pulled the sheet up to his chin. Then I completely submerged myself beneath the covers. It was like a steam room under there, but I had to escape the torment.

After a sleepless night, we rose to a beautiful sunrise with roosters crowing out our window. I turned to Jim, looked at his face, and burst out laughing.

"What are you laughing about?"

"You, your face. You look like a Cyclops!"

"What do you mean?" he asked as he ran his hands

over his face. There was a large red bump in the center of his forehead.

"Oh my God, it feels huge!" He hopped out of bed to look in a mirror.

"That damn mosquito must have been feeding on me all night!" He exclaimed.

CHAPTER 10

The next few weeks were filled with the usual excitement of unpacking and trying to locate needed items from the endless boxes piled in each of the rooms. It was incredibly hot and humid, and I was not accustomed to it. One day, I got something in my eyes. They were burning horribly, and I thought something was terribly wrong. I called for Jim and explained that both of my eyes were on fire and I couldn't take it. He laughed as he told me that sweat burns when it drips into your eyes. As someone who doesn't sweat much, this was a new and unpleasant experience for me. It was dripping down my forehead as we unpacked all the boxes and moved furniture, so I wrapped a bandana around my head to prevent it from getting into my eyes again. I looked like a pirate, which was a fitting costume for our new home in the Caribbean. All that was missing was an eye patch.

I later discovered that September and October are two of the hottest months in St. Thomas. There was no beautiful sea breeze to cool us off; those are known as the Christmas winds, and they cool the islands during the winter months. My only visit to St. Thomas was during the Christmas holidays when the weather was spectacular. What made it even worse was that we had chosen a house that was tucked into the hillside so that it would be safe from hurricanes. Unfortunately, that also protected it from those beautiful sea breezes.

The weeks that followed were lonely for me because Jim returned to the states to work each week. We needed the money because all that we had saved and invested was lost due to the stock market crash after 9/11. I continued to put the house in order and made a home for us while Jim traveled. I didn't expect to be starting our new lives together all by myself. The whole reason for leaving San Francisco was so that Jim would stop traveling for work, and we could finally be together again. Though I was not very happy about it, I understood that we had no choice. No one could have imagined the events of 9/11, nor the many repercussions from such an attack. If Jim needed to travel for his job in order to support us, then that is what he would do. In any case, I was quite used to the routine and fell into my usual patterns. I had plenty to do to keep me busy.

There was so much to learn about life in the Caribbean. There were so many cultural differences that never occurred to me, and the learning curve seemed arduous. For example, I was desperate to be connected to all that was happening stateside, so I promptly went to the cable company to get hooked up. I waited in a long line and, when I finally got to the sales representative, I launched into my request. She looked at me, shook her head, and sucked her teeth loudly. I wasn't sure what that meant, but it wasn't good. After filling out all the paperwork, I was eagerly anticipating hooking up our television and wireless. Then I was told that there were no more cable boxes.

"What do you mean?" I asked.

"Just what I said. There are none left," she responded.

"So when can I get one?"

"I don't know…I suppose when somebody turns one in."

"I don't understand; you won't be getting any new boxes? I have to wait until someone cancels their cable service?"

"That's right, and there is nothing I can do about that."

"But that's absurd!"

She sucked her teeth at me again and turned away. I wasn't happy, and she didn't care. I left there in disbelief. How can they conduct business like this? It's ridiculous that they don't have enough equipment for all their customers. That fact did not seem to bother them at all. That was simply the way business was conducted in St. Thomas, and there was no use in getting worked up about it.

During our country's most significant national crisis, I was without cable and Internet. I was a news junkie, and given what was going on in New York, I was beside myself, not knowing when we might get connected. I was desperate to learn the latest details of the investigations and theories regarding the attacks in New York, D.C., and Pennsylvania. With no recourse, I just hung out in the air-conditioned waiting rooms of the various businesses that I visited to set up utilities and other essential services. I lingered by the televisions just to catch a glimpse of the news. I also went to the Big K-Mart, where I could loiter in the electronics department and watch the latest reports about the attacks. I couldn't visit friends to watch with them because I hadn't met many people yet; I felt pretty isolated. With Jim traveling again, it was quite lonely in our new island paradise, and I couldn't even distract myself by watching TV.

Despite this major disappointment, I followed my morning routine and continued with my list of errands for the day. I took the opportunity to watch the news reports at each stop. Every office or service provider had televisions on the New York news stations. All the locals were glued to them while trying to carry on with their normal routines, trying to make sense of all that had happened. This was my new reality, and I had lots to get done in order to get our lives settled in St. Thomas. But I felt more than frustrated with the long lines and slow business practices. Each encounter I had was fraught with conflict. I couldn't grasp why everyone was so reluctant to help me; I was hurt and wondered why people were so rude to me.

At one point during my first week alone, I found myself at the phone company. As usual, I waited in line for 30 minutes or so, thankful for the air-conditioning and the opportunity to cool down. When my turn came, I stepped up to the counter and stated my business immediately.

"I just moved to the island and need to get phone service. The address is…"

"Good afternoon. How can I help you?" The clerk interrupted.

I was taken aback and paused. She was making a point to say hello to me before taking care of business. So I replied in kind.

"Good afternoon, how are you today?"

"Very well, thank you. So you are new to the island."

With a wry smile, she continued to help me set up our phone service. When we were finished, I made sure to end our encounter politely.

"Thank you very much, ma'am. Have a good day." She smiled at my polite farewell and responded,

"You too, sir. Welcome to St. Thomas."

As I turned to walk out, I overheard the next person in line begin her conversation with "Good afternoon." It finally dawned on me that I had been impolite, totally unaware of this practice. In the Virgin Islands, it is customary to greet people with a good morning or good afternoon before starting your business. That is a simple courtesy on the islands, and it is an important protocol. Violating it is considered rude.

I learned something that day about culture and sensitivity. I had been totally self-absorbed in my own needs, and it was not until my rudeness was cleverly brought to my attention that I began to see beyond myself. The people of St. Thomas were not rude and unfriendly at all. Because of my lack of sensitivity and awareness, I had been the rude party in each of my interactions.

CHAPTER
11

As I continued putting the house together, I would often walk out to the lanai. It offered a welcome respite, looking out at the gorgeous panoramic view that was directly from a postcard. One of the most iconic crescent-shaped beaches on Magens Bay was just below us; the Peterborg peninsula stretches out beyond that with other tiny islands spotting the horizon. The flowering trees and lush foliage in our front yard framed our expansive vista. The brilliant orange blossoms of the flamboyant and the pink and white flowers of the orchid trees displayed their colors distinctly against the azure backdrop of the Atlantic Ocean.

Each room of our home was gracious, with a great deal of light and lofty cathedral ceilings. The living room had a stunning wall built of local blue and gray stone that reached to the roofline. It was magnificent. Beautiful tiles of terra-cotta flooring extended throughout the house, and the arched front doors opened to the massive great room that became home to our Steinway grand piano. The kitchen had cobalt blue tiled counters with a grand island that just called out for guests to gather around it. But first, we had to meet them.

I was in this grand new home alone, while Jim continued to travel back to the U.S. mainland each week for work. Although I hadn't made any friends during those first weeks, the situation began to improve. In the weeks that followed, our realtor and the closing attorney had told their friends about us. Thankfully, a number of them dropped by to introduce themselves. I received each interruption to my painting and unpacking gladly, and I enthusiastically greeted these new friends. Each welcomed us to the island and extended dinner invitations.

Gradually, we began to make connections with a wonderful group of people. Being a musician, I immediately sought out a musical outlet at the University of the Virgin

Islands. Its choir, Polymnia, had an excellent reputation. I called the university and spoke to the director about membership. Since rehearsals were already underway, she was a bit reluctant to let me audition.

"Well, I understand your interest, but not everyone who auditions is accepted into the choir."

"I certainly understand. I was a choir director in San Francisco for many years."

"Is that so? Did you sing as well?"

"Yes, I have a master's degree in voice performance. I'm a tenor." At that, her tone changed completely.

"Oh, well, that is great news. We always need tenors. Can you come to our rehearsal 15 minutes early on Tuesday?"

"Of course! Should I prepare a song?"

The director instructed me to come to the music room at the University with sheet music and a song prepared for the audition. I was looking forward to that evening all week and even drove to the campus a day in advance to be sure I could find it. On the appointed day, I entered the rehearsal room and introduced myself to the director.

"Hello, I'm Mario. We spoke on the phone earlier this week regarding my audition."

"Oh, yes, hello. My name is Lauren; I am the

director."

"I realize that your rehearsals are already in progress, so I just want to tell you how much I appreciate your willingness to let me audition."

"Of course, Mario. Did you mention that you are a choir director as well? Tell me a bit about yourself."

After a short conversation about my musical background, she told me that she could best evaluate my musicianship during the rehearsal.

"I have a song prepared. Would you like to hear that first?"

"No need, I am sure that I will be able to hear you during our rehearsal tonight. Let's chat for a few minutes afterward."

I was only one of two tenors there that evening, so my contribution to the choir was clearly audible. About an hour in, she paused and introduced me to the rest of the choir as the new member of the tenor section. I was elated. Singing with them provided me with an artistic community that fed my creative needs. After a few weeks, I began helping the director during rehearsals and getting to know a small group of musicians to pal around with.

I was thrilled that Polymnia would be performing the

Bach Magnificat in D for their concert the following March. I had sung the piece before and loved every movement of it. At the end of the rehearsal, the director announced the dates for solo auditions. During our conversation afterward, she assured me that I was sure to get one of the tenor solos, especially since I had sung one of them with another choral ensemble. I really felt that I fit in with the choir, and it was certain to become a major social outlet for me.

After rehearsal was over, many of the singers stayed and chatted with one another. Many came to me to introduce themselves and welcome me to the choir. A lovely woman with beautiful blond hair greeted me, "Hi, I'm Kathy. I hear that you're from San Francisco. My husband and I lived there for many years. He was pastor of the Lutheran church on 16th and Dolores Streets." My eyes grew wide as I realized that I recognized her.

"Are you serious? I was the music director at Mission Dolores for the last ten years!"

"Then you must know my husband, Andrew."

"Of course! We celebrated numerous ecumenical services together. How did you end up in St. Thomas?"

"Oh, that is a long story! We will have to get together. I am sure that Andrew would love to see you again."

Mission Dolores Basilica is directly across the street from St. Matthew's Lutheran Church, and we had met on a number of occasions. Kathy and Andrew had two adorable little girls. Andrew was the pastor at Frederick's Lutheran Church in Charlotte Amalie, the second Lutheran church established in the western hemisphere. The four of us struck up an effortless rapport and began to spend more time with each other. Both Kathy and I had been choral directors and music teachers in the San Francisco Bay Area, so we reminisced about our talented choirs and the lack of quality choral music on St. Thomas. It was great to have people who understood the cultural differences that we were experiencing and who could take it all in stride with good humor.

Though we had both been Catholic seminarians in our younger years, Jim and I attended the services at Frederick's Church that following Sunday. The community was not what we were used to at most Catholic churches where people keep a more private space at mass. At Frederick's, we were greeted by everyone who noticed us. We were welcomed, hugged, and drawn into the community. The social gathering after the service was a must, and we were enthusiastically encouraged to try each of the tasty dishes prepared by the parishioners. Kathy introduced me to the organist, who was also the music director at the local private school, where I hoped to get a job. When he heard my name, he exclaimed, "Oh, the tenor!" Over the years, as my teaching and conducting career began to develop, my vocal work seemed to fall to the wayside. It had been so long since I was recognized for my singing voice, and it felt good.

After that Sunday, Jim and I began to attend services at Frederick on a regular basis. It was such an intimate community and provided another means of getting to know people on the island. We quickly became part of the Frederick family. If I ran into parishioners while at the post office in town, they would tell us they missed us if we happened to skip a Sunday.

The atmosphere in the Catholic Church nearby was entirely different. We attended mass there when we first arrived. We hoped that it would offer us a much-needed community of people with whom we could establish friendships. I thought nostalgically about our friends at Mission Dolores Basilica in San Francisco. Over the years, the relationships that we had built became our chosen family. When we walked into the quaint hilltop church on that first Sunday, no one introduced himself or herself to us. That didn't particularly bother us because we were accustomed to that dynamic in most Catholic churches. However, the pastor, who was a young man, was incredibly conservative. I spotted him before mass wearing a long black cassock and a biretta, which is a clerical hat that had been worn by priests before all the changes of the Vatican Council in the 1960s. No one in the states wore clerical garb like that unless they were extremely right-wing. These were people who lived for the "smells and bells" of the old days, using incense and ringing bells at every chance they got. Back in our seminary days, we kept a healthy distance from those characters. I turned and nudged Jim as I pointed him out.

"Get a load of him. Nice outfit!"

"Damn, it must be 95 degrees. He must be melting under there," Jim said.

"Yeah, I can't wait to see what kind of embroidered silk he'll be wearing to say Mass," I responded.

"Well, we're definitely not in Kansas anymore!"

Father Neoconservative did not disappoint; his vestments included layers of white lace topped with a green satin chasuble and embroidered with gold crosses and fleur-de-lis. But the worst part was his horrible homily when he spoke out against evils of letting children read the "Harry Potter" books because they encouraged witchcraft and the belief in magic. This guy was a nut case, and we were turned off immediately. Friends of ours who attended mass there on a regular basis reported that the priest was also vehemently homophobic and often preached against the evils of homosexuality. There was no need for us to return to that church in the future. Not surprisingly, Father Neoconservative left the church a number of years later to live with his boyfriend. They moved off the island to avoid the scandal that inevitably followed. Had he not preached so vehemently against the "gay lifestyle," his decision would not have created so much drama. However, as is so often the case, the most homophobic people are those who can't seem to come to terms with their own sexuality.

CHAPTER 12

Jim and I were slowly beginning to settle into the slower rhythm of life in St. Thomas. We had a small group of new friends with whom we would gather on weekends. Meanwhile, I was busy painting the bedrooms and putting photos and artwork in each room. It took the first two months in St. Thomas to wind down from our hectic city lives and shed our stress. Before we knew it, the time had come to get our dream sailboat.

Both of us were excited about taking possession of the boat that we had purchased months before. While still in San Francisco, we did a great deal of research on various sailboats before we made our final decision. After seeing hundreds of boats at marinas and boat shows, we felt that we had a good sense of what we liked and what was best in our price range. During our first months in St. Thomas, we visited several marinas and looked at the many different boats there. There was such a variety of design styles and gages of equipment; it was clear that there was a great deal to consider when buying a new boat.

During a visit to a boat show in June, we found a 50-foot sailboat that would be large enough to make an ocean voyage. Our plan was to captain and charter the sailboat for tourists visiting St. Thomas. With that in mind, we chose a design that had a spacious area on deck that would allow for numerous guests for day sails as well as sailing from island to island in the Caribbean. It had been months since we had made our purchase, and I could barely remember what our boat looked like. We were both anxious to pick her up. Though she was ready for us in September, we were counseled to wait until the height of the hurricane season had passed before sailing it to the Caribbean. September and October are generally the most active months for hurricanes, so we decided to wait until November.

On November 9, 2001, I flew to Norfolk, Virginia.

From there, we planned to sail to Bermuda and then on to St. Thomas. I had initially hoped that we could follow the coastline until we reached Florida rather than sailing out in the open ocean. The comfort of having land in sight and being close to emergency services was essential to me. The idea of sailing out in the open ocean generated a great deal of anxiety. However, a number of people recommended sailing across to Bermuda; from there, we would have a smooth sail down to the Virgin Islands. Given the flow of the Gulf Stream, which moves north along the U.S. east coast, my original idea of hugging the coastline would have had us fighting the currents for the entire sail. Sailing beyond the Gulf Stream to Bermuda would eliminate that problem and provide for a more efficient route that would take less time. I knew that I had to face my fear of the open ocean, and this was the perfect opportunity to do so.

Jim had gone out a few days ahead of me in order to meet the captain and crew and to take care of a number of errands. He met me at the airport, and we took a taxi to the marina. With all my luggage and gear in hand, I ambled down the dock to our new boat. I recall my excitement the first time I saw her; she was beautiful, a dream come true. We named her Sogno, the Italian word for dream, and as we boarded her, I realized the name was well chosen. I was struck by how spacious and comfortable the deck was; there was plenty of room for passengers to lounge. I could picture us having wine and cheese while on a leisurely sail, watching golden sunsets and feeling the warm breeze on our faces. The cabin down below was just as grand. There were two commodious, over-stuffed leather seats to one side. On the other, there was a banquette of rich tea wood with a generous seating area. The galley was huge with a four-burner cook-top and oven, two refrigerators, and plenty of cabinets for food storage.

There were three sleeping cabins. Those at the stern of the boat were for guests. They both slept two people comfortably and shared the main bathroom and shower. The captain's cabin was at the bow of the boat, and it felt like a suite. As I entered, I passed by the bathroom and shower to see a full queen-sized bed with nightstands and aisles on either side. The backboard had shelving for books and was flanked by two storage compartments. The tea wood finishes all around the cabin were beautiful. This was our cabin, and I couldn't believe that we would be spending two weeks of sailing in this luxury. I was in awe; this was our sailboat; it was truly the boat of our dreams – our dream boat.

Mark and Cheryl drove down from Washington, D.C., that afternoon to wish us well and christen the boat with champagne. Mark tried to smash the bottle on the hull of the boat, but it just bounced off. We laughed and decided to simply pop the cork and pour a bit on her bow. Of course, we drank the rest. That evening, we had a lovely dinner as we described our sailing plan and looked forward to having them visit us in St. Thomas during the holidays. They were such a big part of the whole expedition because Jim and I discovered the wonders of St. Thomas with them the year before. They seemed to be just as excited about our sail as we were.

CHAPTER 13

D aybreak had barely arrived, and I could tell that Jim was anxious to get underway. The hired captain seemed a bit slower and less fastidious than Jim would have liked. The dynamic was strange as I observed the power struggle begin to manifest itself. The captain had many more years of experience and was a really nice guy. Still, Jim was a bit more accurate in planning and had a better understanding of the electronics along with the technical aspects of sailing. So as the journey began, they jockeyed for control in subtle ways. The captain continually asserted himself as the man in charge, and Jim would subtly challenge some of the calculations that Captain Bob had made. There was also another hired crew member who did not seem particularly friendly and was very guarded. I wondered if he was just uncomfortable with the fact that we were gay because he had barely spoken to us since we boarded the boat the previous evening. In that regard, his demeanor did not change much throughout the trip. Another factor that might have affected our group dynamic was the fact that Jim and I were about 25 years younger than either of them. They questioned every opinion or decision we made.

At the crack of dawn, Mark and Cheryl returned for our send-off. They took photos and wished us well. They promised to join us for a sail in St. Thomas in the near future. When the time came, Mark released the dock lines, and as Sogno slowly motored away from our slip, they waved goodbye as we set sail. I couldn't believe that we were actually on our way across the ocean. Mark and Cheryl were so supportive and excited by our expedition that it brought me great comfort. I didn't feel anxious as Sogno motored away from the dock, and I watched them get smaller and smaller as we continued to wave goodbye. They faded into nothingness along with the marina and buildings along the shore. Before us lay the vastness of the Atlantic Ocean, and all I could see around me was gray water.

As the first day wore on, the chilly wind got under my skin. It was early November, and it was cold. I took comfort in the fact that we would cross the Gulf Stream overnight, at which point the temperature would rise, and the waters would warm up quite a bit. I anticipated that this was going to be a challenge for me because, since childhood, I had always feared the open ocean. It was ominous as I looked out over cheerless gray waves as far as the eye could see. I had never been out on a boat of any sort where I could not see land. The mere thought of being in water whose depth was greater than the meter could measure made me more than a little anxious. The last depth reading was over three thousand feet deep, and we were clearly beyond that. Although I was afraid, I believed that this would be my great challenge and that I would finally overcome my irrational fears.

Each crew member had assigned shifts at the helm, so there was no escaping the challenge. Though I was anxious, I knew that my sailing experience in the high winds of San Francisco Bay had trained me well. I understood the concepts of capturing the wind and surfing the larger waves; I knew what to do. However, a relevant detail that never occurred to me as we charted our voyage across the ocean was that we would be sailing 24 hours a day until we arrived in Bermuda. There are no ports to sail into or safe harbors in which to drop anchor out in the open ocean; the waters are thousands of feet deep. That fact alone stirred a profound fear within me. I soon realized that this sail would be much more difficult than I had imagined.

It took about an hour and a half to get out of the Chesapeake Bay past Cape Henry. At this point, we put up modest sails and continued to motor. As we were leaving the Chesapeake Bay, we noticed a great deal of variance between the readings on the magnetic compass, the GPS, and the autohelm. This variance made the autohelm inoperable, which meant that we would need to hand steer until we could find the origin of the problem. We figured that all of the national security equipment in use in Norfolk could be the cause of the problem with the three instruments.

This made navigating quite challenging. We would have to continue our sail to Bermuda without the help of the autohelm. That meant that we would have to chart our course manually on the maps down below and use the compass as our guide. We were all frustrated and knew that this would make it much more challenging to navigate at night. Fortunately, as we got further into the Atlantic, the

GPS and the magnetic compass came into sync. But the autohelm remained in error, and the high seas made it impossible to spin the compass in order to reset it. We just needed to accept that fact and do the best we could without it.

I was the cook for the journey, primarily because I hate sandwiches, and I like to prepare warm foods for both lunch and dinner. Jim affectionately referred to me as the galley wench. Captain Bob and David had no idea what to make of that, but we didn't care. I enjoy cooking, and since I felt a bit inadequate when it came to sailing in blue water (the open ocean), it was a comfortable role for me to play. We had provisioned the boat with all sorts of food, and I had most of the menus planned for the three-and-a-half-day sail. We planned on re-stocking when we got to Bermuda, before continuing to St. Thomas.

As the first day waned, I cooked supper for the crew and cleaned up. I was grateful that Jim took my afternoon shift at the helm, but I knew that he preferred being up on deck rather than down below. Being on deck warded off the seasickness for most of us. It was freezing that day, and we all suffered during our shifts. We were motor sailing the entire way in order to make more headway. With our sails up, catching every bit of wind, and the motor moving us along, we were averaging about nine knots. It was an excellent speed for a sailboat of this size. The speed that a boat can travel is directly related to the length of the hull. We were sailing close to the maximum speed for our boat.

Up to that point in my life, I had never gotten seasick. But that morning, I stayed below for hours, trying to keep out of the cold. I was reading an epic novel about Greenwich Village in New York City during the early twentieth century, and I was deeply immersed in the story when nausea hit me. I immediately went up on deck to get some fresh air and stare at the horizon. This is a common remedy that is often recommended to balance one's equilibrium, and it worked; my seasickness passed quickly. The rest of the guys stayed on deck for most of the day, and I stayed with them so as not to tempt fate. But that would fail us once evening came.

I had a delicious menu planned for that night: curried coconut chicken with snow peas, carrots, peppers, and mushrooms served over rice. I was busily chopping vegetables and frying them up. The boat was rocking quite a bit as we neared the Gulf Stream, but I kept my wits about me as I balanced the pots and pans while trying to keep them on the cooktop. The stove was gimbaled, so it stayed level as the boat swayed. Unfortunately, I did not. I began to feel the first signs of seasickness, and nausea passed over me in waves. I knew that I should just go on deck to get some fresh air until it passed, but I was almost done with cooking, and I figured that I could fight it off until I finished up. That was a mistake. I was ultimately able to finish cooking, but I never got to eat. I ran to the bathroom and vomited violently. My head was swimming, and my stomach was doing flip-flops; I was down for the count.

The second to fall to seasickness was David. He was a seasoned sailor so, it took him by surprise. Unfortunately, he was unable to rise to take his shift at the helm in order to relieve Jim, who had meticulously planned the schedule. We were each to take a two-hour shift at the helm, followed by two more hours on deck during the next person's shift. This would ensure that there would always be at least two people on deck just in case something happened, or if the person at the helm needed help with anything. That would also allow the second person some time to rest before going down below when the next shift started. I depended upon that rotation because I was terrified of being at the helm alone, especially in the middle of the night. Jim took David's shift, which was from 10:00 p.m. to midnight; his own shift was to run from 12-2 a.m. Since we were already down a man and I was feeling better, I came up for my shift at 2 a.m. Jim was bleary-eyed and completely wiped out. He looked miserable as he harnessed me in.

"OK, Mario, you're all hooked in. How are you feeling?"

"Physically, I feel fine. My head and stomach are back to normal. But I'm anxious about my shift."

"You'll do just fine. You know what you're doing. Listen, I just did four hours straight, and I am shivering out here and completely wiped out. I really need to get some sleep. Do you think you can handle this on your own? I just want to go below to warm up and rest."

How could I say no? He looked miserable, and I realized that he would be of no comfort to me in his present state. It was better for him to get some rest. So rather than stay on deck during my shift, Jim double-checked my harness and went below to sleep. It was a starless night, and I felt as if the darkness was closing in on me with every wave that hit. I was terrified.

We should have been able to set our course and let the autohelm take the lead. That would have made my nighttime shift easier. However, due to the fact that the autohelm was not functioning properly, the only way to guide the boat was by manually steering while watching the compass. It floated and spun around in its casing. With each wave that hit, our course seemed to change. Although I had the coordinates and knew where to direct the boat, I couldn't quite get a handle on it.

The Gulf Stream created miles of turbulent waters, and there didn't seem to be a steady pattern with regard to the direction from which the waves approached. I continually felt as if each one threw us off course. I recall desperately trying to correct our course, and in doing so, I overcompensated and had to correct it again. I was in an endless cycle of moving starboard to port, port to starboard. My fingers grew white as I gripped the helm as tightly as I could. With no ambient light, I was sailing blind. I felt completely disoriented because it seemed that the boat was spinning in circles. Apparently, this is a common occurrence when sailing at night; there is no focal point that a sailor can use to orient himself, so the waves create the illusion of spinning.

I was completely alone on the deck of a 50-foot sailboat in the middle of the ocean. This was not how I imagined that I would overcome my fear. As the waves came at me from every direction, I was simply reacting to each hit as the boat would ascend to the crest of the wave and slam down in the belly of the next. The noise was deafening; it sounded as if the hull itself was cracking apart. The burst of noise at the moment the hull struck the sea below caused me to shiver in fear. The creaking fiberglass and metal thundered their displeasure at each crashing fall as if the boat would shatter into pieces at any moment. I feared that I was doing some real damage to our brand new sailboat, but I didn't know how to remedy the situation. Every time I felt the boat rise, I braced myself for inevitable disaster. My heart trembled in my chest and my grip on the helm tightened such that my fingers began to cramp. There are very few moments in my life that I have felt that I was in over my head, but those long hours at the helm filled me with dread. I was well beyond my expertise or comfort zone. I was trapped with no recourse. Even if I shouted for help, I would not be heard over the roaring wind and waves.

As time passed by, however, my anxiety lessened. I began to anticipate the approaching waves and gradually learned to adjust accordingly. I began to grow more comfortable as I felt the hull of the boat rise. I turned it slightly so that the approach was at a 45-degree angle rather than hitting the swell head-on. When I did that, Sogno smoothly sailed down the other side at an angle; it was more akin to surfing than sailing. Without the use of sight, I became more aware of my other senses and was slowly able to adjust to the darkness. More importantly, I began to feel the movement of the sea and was able to guide us through the night. I was never more grateful than when my replacement came to relieve me after two very long and lonely hours at the helm. After he was harnessed in, I made myself comfortable in a protected corner of the deck and tried to get warm. Though weary, I felt good about myself and had a sense of accomplishment. I had not only survived without any help, but I maintained our course and advanced toward our destination.

After my two hours on deck after my shift, I returned to the comfort of the captain's cabin, where I snuggled under the covers with Jim. I could finally rest my mind and relieve the tension in my muscles after my hours at the helm. No sooner did I get myself settled when we crested a wave, and the bow of the boat came crashing down. Jim and I were both thrown into the air, knocked our heads on the ceiling, and then slammed back down onto the bed. This pattern continued for the remainder of the night. The creaking and groaning of the hull was amplified in the V berth, right at the tip of the boat. Sounds echoed loudly in our quarters, and the wind howled through the cracks.

At that point, we realized that the forward cabin, our captain's cabin, was the rockiest area of the boat. We came to the conclusion that with seas so rough, we would not be able to use it for sleep. That did not sit well with me for a number of reasons. The only alternative was to sleep around the table in the main cabin, which provided no privacy. I was already ill at ease with David's cool attitude towards us and did not feel comfortable sleeping out in the open. In addition, because of the direction of our sail and the prevailing winds, the boat was tipped toward the starboard side at a 45-degree angle, dumping us off the sleeping area. We continually slid off the banquet and onto the floor. We had to hook our arms around the mast poll in order to stay still. Having to stay alert enough to hold onto the mast made it impossible to sleep. After our exhausting shifts on deck, we needed restorative sleep. But we were out of options—there were no other places to sleep. We were resigned to the fact that we would not be able to fully sleep for the rest of the trip to Bermuda.

CHAPTER 14

The morning of the second day dawned with sunny weather and steady winds. We were now over 300 nautical miles from the east coast of the United States, and there was no land in sight. The winds were at our nose, so we continued to motor-sail. I greeted my time at the helm with much more confidence than I had on the first day. After my accomplishment the night before, I felt more confident about my skills as a sailor. I had done it on my own, alone on deck. Not bad for a person who had a significant phobia of the open ocean. While resting on the deck, I pulled out my Nikon SLR camera and began to take photos of the turbulent sea as Sogno easily cut through the waves. It was a good day of sailing, and we made significant headway toward Bermuda.

As a crew, we settled into a comfortable rhythm. We each took our shifts, and I continued to cook dinners. Captain Bob and David became a bit friendlier, and Jim busied himself with learning every aspect of our new sailboat. One morning as I came down from my shift on deck, I spotted Captain Bob propped between the two countertops in the galley. The angle of the boat was approximately 45 degrees, so it was a challenge for anyone to stand straight and still. He was having his breakfast, a bowl of cereal resting upon his generous belly with a trail of Cheerios leading up his chest and milk drops dangling from his chin. I thought, "Now this is an image that instills confidence. If this is our Captain, we are in serious trouble."

As days passed, Jim got more and more agitated at the condition of the boat. He has always been a neat freak, but seeing how poorly kept our new boat was, he was beside himself. He went into the main bathroom, and his ire reached its limit. There was dried urine all over the walls and a pool of it on the floor. It was disgusting. He sat both Captain Bob and David down to explain that they had to sit down when they went to the head. With the boat rocking and slamming down on the waves, there was no way to stand and get all of the waste into the bowl. They scoffed at him and assured him that they would take better care. But we knew that they were simply placating him.

The sail was taking much longer than expected due to the direction of the wind and the foul weather. By the fourth day, we had hit more rough weather. The winds were steady at 30 to 35 knots, with 15 to 20-foot seas and heavy rain. We were never able to cut the engine and sail without being under power. While I was at the helm, Jim decided to reef in the sail due to the wind. We had too much of the sail out for such high winds.

The tension on the main furling line was high, and the splice in the line snapped, causing the entire sail to come out, flapping noisily in the blowing wind. The only choice was to pull in the mainsail by hand. Jim took a tether and snapped it to the lines leading forward from the mast, and, with a winch handle in his hand, he climbed onto the upper deck to the mast. Even with the winch handle in place, he could only get a quarter of a turn on the ratchet. I could not believe that he was on deck in high seas trying to reef in the sail by hand. Against the heavy winds and waves breaking over the bow, we were both getting soaked. He lost his footing several times as the waves crashed over the bow and rushed under his feet. We were terrified, and I yelled down below for help, but no one heard. The noise was roaring all around us; the crashing waves that used to bring me peace while walking on the seashore were now rumbling like an earthquake. As the winds blew through the sails, all the lines created such a clamor of flapping canvas and clanging metal that we could not hear each other over the thunderous din.

The wind and rain were relentless, and the waves continued to crash onto the bow of the boat. Jim was taking a serious pounding on deck, and without his harness, he would not have been able to hang on. Eventually, Captain Bob came up and gave him a hand. We got the sail reefed in so that it would not catch as much wind, and we changed tack. It did not help as much as we had hoped; it was still rough sailing. But the crisis seemed to be over.

That night the weather worsened. The wind was so strong, and rains were so heavy that it hurt as it pelted against our faces and hands. The wind held steady at 37 knots, and the gusts registered over 40 knots. While Jim and I were on our shifts that evening, a line snapped once again; this time, it was to the mainsail. Jim attempted to sew it back together using wire and thread but had little success. As we were pulling in the jib (front sail), the line got tangled, and the line to the stay broke free of its catch. The metal fastener was flying freely and banging against the hull of the boat. It seemed like everything was going wrong. We could barely concentrate on fixing one problem when another would occur. Once again, Jim was on the bow of the boat trying to ratchet in the sail by hand when he got knocked over by a 20-foot wave crashing onto him. Even though he was tethered to the boat, he was nearly washed overboard. Somehow, he got himself back on his feet and continued to bring the sail down; persistence was the only option. He had to get the sail lowered in the heavy wind and high seas.

After our shifts were over, Captain Bob and David continued to call Jim up from his all-too-brief rest in order to adjust the sails. Neither of them had the agility to climb onto the bow in that weather. By the end of the evening, we had survived the latest crisis only to discover that we were now more than 30 miles further from our destination. It was day five of the sail, and we were supposed to have arrived in Bermuda by that time. Instead, we were days behind schedule and weary from the last 24 hours of crisis management.

I had to take another night shift that night from 2:00

to 4:00 a.m. I was certainly more comfortable than I had been at the beginning of the week, and I was becoming much more confident in my sailing skills. Still, I was miserable. After five difficult days at sea, I regretted my decision to come along on the journey. My dower mood was unmistakable. Jim tried his best to comfort me, but we had much more pressing concerns. After my shift, I went below to wake the next person in line. I had just descended the steps and was standing at the bottom. As I let go of the handrail, we hit another huge wave. I was tossed up into the air, snapped backward, and landed squarely on my lower back. I felt and heard it crack. I saw blue and white flashes behind my eyes as I hit the floor. With the wind knocked out of me, I lay on the floor in excruciating pain. I couldn't even call for help. The clamor of the crashing waves and high winds made it nearly impossible to be heard. Jim rested only a few feet away, and even he didn't hear me fall. I had seriously injured my back and could not move. I let myself rest on the floor until the pain abated somewhat, then I slowly turned onto my side as I steadied myself on the stairs. I hobbled over to the banquette and managed to lie on my back. I knew that I would not be able to sail for the next few days because I could barely move. It would prove to be an additional challenge for the crew to carry on with fewer members.

The next night the seas were just as rough, and we were continuing to lose ground on our destination. We were now 60 miles further from Bermuda. At one point, the instrument panel went dark. Jim shut off all of the instruments and restarted them. They all came back except for the navigation. It started to work intermittently, and he suspected a bad connection. He disassembled the helm to assess the wiring and remedy the problem. When he removed the cup holders and lifted the cover to the binnacle, smoke came billowing out. Through the smoke, he could see that there was an electrical fire. About three inches of the wire (all three leads) were burned and glowing red. He then noticed a small fire in the junction block where the autohelm is connected to the GPS. He was frustrated by the poor workmanship and was quite colorful in the language he used to express his anger. His hands were wet, and the electrical coils continually slipped through his fingers. Despite the rain and wind, he was able to rewire them. Thankfully they began to work again, and there was a collective sigh of relief when the monitor glowed with power displaying much of the necessary data needed for our sail.

The weather continued to deteriorate so we decided

to pull in all the sails and hove to, which means that we just stopped sailing and let the boat drift. And drift it did. By morning we were 20 nautical miles off course. These constant setbacks were beginning to add up. The frustration that we all felt was mounting, and the fatigue from physical exertion and lack of sleep was showing in each of us. Each night, Captain Bob used the satellite phone to call his wife and get the latest weather reports. Oddly, they always predicted calm conditions and favorable winds. None of us could understand how our experience at sea was so diametrically opposed to the weather reports we received.

I recall feeling numb to the constant bad news. I couldn't absorb the continual blows we received. I am sure that my defense mechanisms had kicked into gear and were protecting me from despair. If I had let myself feel the mounting frustration, I'm not sure I would have been able to function normally. It was a choice; we had no control over the weather or the mechanical malfunctions. All we could do was use our knowledge to move forward with the ever-changing conditions. Looking back upon how much emotion was repressed during that journey, I am struck by how resilient the human psyche is. Each of us pressed onward and did what was necessary. There was no complaining or moaning about each crisis. We met each with the necessary level of concern but did not let our emotions cloud our judgment. Rather than becoming immobilized by our misfortune, I let the numbness anesthetize me enough so that I could do what had to be done.

CHAPTER 15

By day eight, we awoke to sunny skies and warmer weather. The winds were still at our nose, and the seas were still choppy, so we continued to motor-sail. It was the first day without a crisis or dangerous weather conditions. The motor sailing worked to our advantage, and by the end of the day, we were approximately 25 nautical miles from Bermuda. On the ninth day of sailing, the seas were finally calm enough to adjust the autohelm. This requires the boat to spin in a full circle in order to calibrate it with the compass. It was a success, and we were encouraged that we would finally be able to set our direction and let the boat take the lead. Early that morning, I was sitting on deck with Captain Bob when I spotted a tiny bump at the horizon. I turned to Bob and asked, "Is that Bermuda over there, or am I just imagining things?" He grabbed the binoculars to have a look and let out a cheer.

"You are the first to spot land! Yes, indeed, Mario, that's Bermuda."

I shouted to the guys down below.

"Bermuda is in sight! Come on up."

They both bounced up the stairs with hopeful anticipation.

"How long do you think it will take us to get there, Jim?"

"It will all depend on the wind direction, but we should be there late this afternoon."

I was hoping that we would arrive sooner than that. Now that it was in sight, I just wanted to be there already. The atmosphere on the boat had changed completely. All four of us began to joke about the various crises we had encountered and dreamed of the first thing each of us would do once on dry land. The end was in sight.

We decided to cut the engine to preserve fuel because our trip had taken five days longer than planned. We had to make sure that we had enough fuel to motor into the harbor once we got to Bermuda. As usual, the wind direction did not cooperate, so we spent the remainder of the day tacking back and forth toward our destination. Now that land was in sight, we were all anxious to get there as quickly as possible. However, it would take eight long hours to reach the harbor.

When we finally got to the entrance of the harbor, the sun was setting, and its golden rays sparkled on the calm waters. It looked like a mirror; the only ripples in the water were coming from us. The buildings that lined each side of the harbor glowed with the amber light of sunset. Anchored sailboats bobbed peacefully on their moorings and reflected the hues of the setting sun. The warm clanging of the buoy bell echoed faintly in the distance and seemed to welcome us into the safe harbor of St. George, Bermuda. It was such a beautiful sight that each of us was silent as we slowly motored to our marina. It was the calm after the storm.

As we approached the marina, I threw out the bumpers and prepared the lines. When I hopped onto the dock to tie us up, my legs felt wobbly, and it took a while to get my balance back. Jim and Captain Bob went directly to the marina office to register while David and I gathered up all our trash and straightened out the boat. Once all the paperwork was taken care of, and we were settled, Jim and I grabbed our towels and ran to the marina facilities.

We were desperate to take a hot shower on dry land. The salt was deeply embedded in our hair and caked on our skin. Every scrape or cut had been immersed in saltwater for days as the spray from the ocean wicked into our clothing and under the foul weather gear. So many of our minor wounds were inflamed from the constant irritation of the saltwater. We craved the feel of the soothing warm shower on our battered bodies. The marina had a coin-controlled shower, so we had to add money By day eight, we awoke to sunny skies and warmer weather. The winds were still at our nose, and the seas were still choppy, so we continued to motor-sail. It was the first day without a crisis or dangerous weather conditions. The motor sailing worked to our advantage, and, by the end of the day, we were approximately 25 nautical miles from Bermuda. On the ninth day of sailing, the seas were finally calm enough to adjust the autohelm. This requires the boat to spin in a full circle in order to calibrate it with the compass. It was a success, and we were encouraged that we would finally be able to set our direction and let the boat take the lead. Early that morning, I was sitting on deck with Captain Bob when I spotted a tiny bump at the horizon. I turned to Bob and asked, "Is that Bermuda over there, or am I just imagining things?" He grabbed the binoculars to have a look and let out a cheer.

"You are the first to spot land! Yes, indeed, Mario, that's Bermuda."

I shouted to the guys down below.

"Bermuda is in sight! Come on up."

They both bounced up the stairs with hopeful anticipation.

"How long do you think it will take us to get there, Jim?"

"It will all depend on the wind direction, but we should be there late this afternoon."

I was hoping that we would arrive sooner than that. Now that it was in sight, I just wanted to be there already. The atmosphere on the boat had changed completely. All four of us began to joke about the various crises we had encountered and dreamed of the first thing each of us would do once on dry land. The end was in sight.

We decided to cut the engine to preserve fuel because our trip had taken five days longer than planned. We had to make sure that we had enough fuel to motor into the harbor once we got to Bermuda. As usual, the wind direction did not cooperate, so we spent the remainder of the day tacking back and forth toward our destination. The following eight hours could not have been longer. The beautiful island of Bermuda seemed to be teasing us as we slowly made our way towards it.

When we finally got to the entrance of the harbor, the sun was setting, and its golden rays sparkled on the calm waters. It looked like a mirror; the only ripples in the water were coming from us. The buildings that lined each side of the harbor glowed with the amber light of sunset. Anchored sailboats bobbed peacefully on their moorings and reflected the hues of the setting sun. The warm clanging of the buoy bell echoed faintly in the distance and seemed to welcome us into the safe harbor of St. George, Bermuda. It was such a beautiful sight that each of us was silent as we slowly motored to our marina. It was the calm after the storm.

As we approached the marina, I threw out the bumpers and prepared the lines. When I hopped onto the dock to tie us up, my legs felt wobbly, and it took a while to get my balance back. Jim and Captain Bob went directly to the marina office to register while David and I gathered up all our trash and straightened out the boat. Once all the paperwork was taken care of, and we were settled, Jim and I grabbed our towels and ran to the marina facilities.

We were desperate to take a hot shower on dry land. The salt was deeply embedded in our hair and caked on our skin. Every scrape or cut had been immersed in saltwater for days as the spray from the ocean wicked into our clothing and under the foul weather gear. So many of our minor wounds were inflamed from the constant irritation of the saltwater. We craved the feel of the soothing warm shower on our battered bodies. The marina had a coin-controlled shower, so we had to add money continually to keep the water flowing. After nine full days without showers, it seemed that we couldn't scrub hard enough or long enough to get the stink off of us. We scrubbed and scrubbed until we could no longer sense the odor. Though we had to run out of the stall to add coins continually, we declared that it was the best shower of our lives.

The following day was spent repairing our new sailboat after its maiden voyage. We were able to access our email at a local cybercafé and found out where we could get supplies. We needed to get diesel, clean the boat, and do laundry. In addition, we needed some long overdue rest and relaxation.

That day, the generator malfunctioned and shut off;

there was no water getting to the cooling system. Jim pulled off the impeller cover to find that the impeller was burned. Upon closer inspection, he discovered that the generator had pulled off of its mount and needed to be repositioned and bolted down. Then we worked on the VHF to ascertain why it was not transmitting. We untangled the power wires from the antenna wire and inspected the connection at the mast base. The connection was sloppy, so we cleaned it up to ensure that there was no grounding to the shield. After that, there was a significant improvement to the VHF transmission capabilities. The sails had to be repaired, and the GPS and autohelm needed to be rewired. As it turned out, of the many boats caught in the awful weather that week, ours seemed to have sustained the least amount of damage. Jim and I both felt that we had a great sailboat and that it had come through with flying colors. The other sailors in the marina told similar horror stories of the sail across the ocean, and we spent a good bit of time commiserating with them as we shared our experiences.

The following day was Thanksgiving. To mark it, we ate at a local restaurant and planned the week ahead. We had spent two days recovering and getting Sogno ready for the final leg of the journey. From then on, we would be sailing in warm waters, and we were all looking forward to a relaxing sail. Everyone told us that we would see all sorts of sea-life and that it would likely be a very comfortable sail to St. Thomas. Within hours of setting sail the following morning, the temperatures began to rise, and we could feel the breeze become warmer. The ocean had a different hue than the mid-Atlantic; it was a lighter blue color and seemed more inviting. Jim was excited about the final leg of the trip.

"Mario, we are going to see some beautiful sights on this part of the sail. There will be fish of all kinds, dolphins, and possibly whales. You're going to want your camera at the ready."

We looked toward the most beautiful part of the sailing trip with great anticipation, and the first day out did not disappoint. The breeze was warm with the wind at our back; the sun was shining brightly, and we made excellent time. At one point, Jim spotted something leaping out of the water, "Look, look there, dolphins!"

"Wow!" I exclaimed, "I've never seen anything like that before. They are beautiful."

There was a pod of them frolicking to our port side, leaping out of the water and back down again. They seemed to be dancing with the waves as they accompanied us along our way. It was truly beautiful to watch their graceful swimming and simple joy. They stayed with us for a long time, yet none of us tired of watching them.

Sunday night brought high seas and heavy winds once again, but we were still sailing wing to wing with the wind at our backs. It is important to keep a steady course with the sails out in opposite directions. If you allow the wind to get too far to the other side of the sail, the boom will swing all the way around with a loud crash. At about 2:00 a.m., David was at the helm for his shift. Having completed his time on deck, Jim was just settling in for the night when all of a sudden, there was a shattering bang as the boom slammed to the other side. Sogno lurched forward and began to spin around in circles.

Jim leapt up the stairs to complain about David's lack of concentration and carelessness in letting the boom swing around; David exclaimed that he could not steer the boat. Jim took over and realized that the rudder was not responding as Sogno spun in circles in the waves. The sails were flapping in the wind, and the lines were getting pulled in all directions. The boom and rigging were banging from side to side, and the clatter was alarming.

By this point, we were all on deck trying to figure out

what to do. After a number of fruitless attempts to get Sogno under control, we decided to heave to for the night. We could not fix the problem in the darkness with the high seas and the pitching of the vessel. Jim locked the wheel to full port rudder and backwinded the jib to port with about one-eighth of the jib out and about one-eighth of the mainsail out. Due to the limited steering capability, Sogno continued to steer into the wind maintaining a course of 330 degrees at about 1.5 – 2.5 knots. We turned off the engine and left the steaming lights on so that we could be seen if another vessel should come across our path. We bunked down for a fitful night as the waves were pitching the vessel to 30 and 40 degrees. All of the items in the cabin were being thrown back in forth in the cabinets and off of the shelves. Between the pitching of the boat and items crashing onto the floor, we got very little sleep.

By 5:30 a.m., we were all up and trying to find a solution to our steering problem. Jim decided that the only way to find out why the helm would not control the rudder was to dive under the boat and inspect the mechanism. That seemed crazy to me, given that we were being tossed about like a beanbag. The seas were still approximately 20 feet, and we could see the stern of the boat bouncing in and out of the waves. He got himself ready with a life jacket and harness to tether himself to the boat.

Jim looked out at the turbulent ocean and paused. Fear was painted all over his face.

"What's the matter, Jim? Are you feeling all right?" I asked.

"I can feel my heart beating so hard that I can barely catch my breath."

"Slow down, Jim. Just take a deep breath."

"My chest is really tight, and my head is pounding," he replied.

"OK, stop for a minute. Let's think this through," I said.

"Once I dive in, how will I keep steady? There's nothing to hold on to."

Captain Bob chimed in. "Then how will we figure out what the problem is?"

Jim turned to me.

"Mario, what if I get in the water, dive under the boat, and it comes crashing down on my head? It could kill me."

"Then don't go, Jim. The last thing we need right now is for you to get hurt or worse. There's got to be some other way to figure out what is wrong,"

"I agree, but I don't know what else to do," he exclaimed.

It was not a smart idea to jump off the boat in such high seas; that plan had to be eliminated. The four of us were gathered on deck, and I asked, "So, what is the next step?"

"Maybe the guy who sold you the boat can give us some advice. Maybe something is jammed, and he can talk us through some sort of fix," Captain Bob suggested.

I went below to search for his telephone number. Neither of us could remember where it was, so I looked through all of the documentation from the boat. His information was nowhere to be found. After a moment of panic, it dawned on me that it must have been on Jim's cell phone. I hadn't even thought of that since we had no cell service out at sea. I had to power it up and found it in his recent calls. Jim got the satellite phone and began to dial. We had hoped that perhaps there was something we were missing and that there was an easy fix to the problem.

Thankfully, our salesman was in the office, and Jim began to explain the problem. His first suggestion was to dive below the stern and inspect the rudder. When Jim described the dangerous weather conditions, the man said that there was no way for him to know what had gone wrong without more information. He then suggested that we drag large buckets on either side of the boat to provide balance and drag. This wouldn't engage the rudder, but it would prevent the boat from bobbing aimlessly in the high seas. Just a side note, how many large buckets does one store on a boat making an ocean voyage? We had two kitchen-sized buckets in a locker in order to clean the deck and hull. With the high seas, there was little chance that this solution would yield the desired results. Jim, who is generally very measured and calm, was visibly irritated with him.

"So you are saying that you have no idea why we might have lost steering capability, and you have no other solution other than dragging buckets? Thanks for your help."

The salesman tried to get Jim to continue on toward St. Thomas with our sailboat in its compromised condition, to which Jim replied that we would do the best we could, given the circumstances. He then hung up.

Looking back on it, there were two plausible theories as to why the rudder wasn't functioning. Both had to do with hitting something. But what could we possibly hit in 5,000 feet of water? Apparently, it is not uncommon for shipping containers to fall off ships during rough weather.

Many of them will float just under the surface until all of the oxygen leaks out before they sink to the bottom of the sea. If that were the case, it would have been impossible for any of us to spot or avoid it with the huge waves crashing over the bow. An alternate theory is that we might have hit a sleeping whale. When they sleep, they remain buoyant and float near the surface so that they can get oxygen quickly when their levels get low. In either case, if we had hit one of them, we could have damaged the rudder.

We agreed that we needed to call the Coast Guard and inform them of our predicament. Captain Bob got on the satellite phone and made the call. He described the situation and gave them our coordinates. They alerted us that there was a tropical depression forming southwest of our position, and stormy weather developing over Bermuda. They asked if we would abandon the vessel if emergency rescue assistance were provided. We evaluated the life and death potential of our situation and decided that we were not at that point yet. We were instructed to call the Coast Guard back in about 30 minutes. They would then update us regarding the possibility of getting a salvage company to come to our rescue and tow the boat to St. Thomas or Puerto Rico.

We continued to discuss the options. Jim and I were less inclined to sail the vessel to St. Thomas, given that our present position was 450 nautical miles away, and Sogno was in an extremely crippled condition. While we had 150 gallons of water and about 120 gallons of diesel fuel onboard, we only had provisions for four or five days. We contacted the US Coast Guard after 30 minutes and were informed that no salvage company would come so far out to sea from either Bermuda or Puerto Rico. We were then asked to check in with the Coast Guard on a three-hour schedule. By that time, our discussion was very animated. I felt that I was out of my league with regard to fixing the steering issue. I knew that my sailing skills were pretty good, but I had no idea how to address an issue like this. As the conversation continued, a ship was spotted about three and a half nautical miles away.

The Coast Guard encouraged us to accept assistance from the ship. Through our numerous calls to them, it became clear that we were in dire circumstances. We had to consider the worsening weather due to a hurricane to our southwest and storms brewing off the coast of Bermuda. We knew that we should make contact with the ship's captain. In maritime law, the nearest ship is obligated to rescue any vessel in distress. The Coast Guard contacted the ship that we spotted, and we were told to wait for a call.

While we waited for the ship to make contact, we reached a consensus that, if we could get a tow to either Bermuda or the Virgin Islands, we would take the assistance. This was based on a number of factors, but the ultimate concern was to protect our lives. In the state that Sogno was in, we believed that we wouldn't be able to make more than two to three knots with optimal conditions. That would mean that the trip would take at least eight days. This was assuming that the winds would continue from the northeast and that the seas would subside. If the winds were coming from the east as the trade winds do, it would be impossible to steer the vessel on a beam reach, which means sailing with the wind at a 90-degree angle to the boat. We didn't have enough food for eight more days, and it was likely that we would still need to be rescued.

The seas were now 25 feet high, and we were concerned that the boat would be breached by the waves. The fact that commercial salvage companies would not come out to our location led us to believe that the safe and reasonable approach was to attempt a tow from a willing vessel.

CHAPTER
16

Not long after our call to the Coast Guard, the captain of the freighter made contact with us and began to head in our direction. He suggested that they use their crane to lift Sogno out of the water and lay her on their deck.

"How are you going to get a hold of it?" Jim asked. "It doesn't have a hook on the top of the mast like a Christmas ornament, and it has a point on the bottom, so you can't just place it on your deck."

The captain laughed.

"Oh, don't you worry. We'll figure out some way to

save your boat. We will contact you when we spot you. Just stay safe until you hear from us."

In the meantime, we continued to secure all our equipment and got ready to get off. We were all busily preparing Sogno for the arriving ship. All loose items were placed in locked cabinets. We tied the dinghy engine, which hung off the stern of the boat, tightly to its mount and stored seat cushions from the deck in one of the sleeping cabins below. During these preparations, David had begun to lose it; he was having a significant anxiety attack and was spinning out of control.

"How are we going to get off the boat? The seas are so high. There is no way they'll be able to rescue us. We could die. What was I thinking? I should never have let you convince me to do this, Bob!"

Captain Bob kept him on deck and tried to calm him down.

"Don't worry, David. They do this sort of thing all the time. We're going to be fine. Once we're on the ship, all of this will be behind us. Think about the look on your wife's face when you tell her you were rescued at sea!"

Jim and I were down below, gathering all our documents and securing everything. All of a sudden, Jim looked out the portal and saw a wall of Rustoleum red; the freighter was only 60 feet away. With the seas as high as they were and Sogno having no sails up, they were unable to see us until they were nearly on top of us. Jim leapt up the gangway to see that they had put the ship in full reverse. That caused the bull-nose of the hull to lift itself directly out of the water and rise up. It looked like an angry sea monster rising from the depths.

The immediate reversal of a ship that size created a huge suction of water towards the freighter. We were caught in it, and a massive rush of water sucked us right into its hull. Within seconds, our 60-foot mast collided with the side of the ship. We heard an ear-piercing bang as the support lines, or struts failed and thrashed around us. The mast snapped in two as it lifted up and away from Sogno. Jim looked up and saw it coming back down onto our boat. The mast pierced the top of the main cabin, missing Jim by no more than a foot. It was as if it were all happening in slow motion. He froze in fear when he realized how close it had come to impaling him. The ship was going to sink us before we would ever be rescued. We were all frantically trying to stay out of harm's way and stay alive.

The freighter turned dangerously during the rescue

effort, with its hull against the crashing waves. There was a concerted effort to right the ship and get her balanced as it began to bob back and forth unsteadily. Sogno was still afloat, and, remarkably, none of us were injured by the initial collision. But each of us was shell-shocked as we waited for further instructions from the ship's captain. They threw us a towline, which we secured to the starboard winches. This placed us alongside the hull of the ship. Due to the pitching of both vessels and the 15-foot seas, there were numerous collisions between the two boats. Our initial intention was to remain on Sogno while she was being towed. But after all the damage that she sustained, we decided that it would be safer to board the rescue ship. Sogno was being tossed up and down alongside the freighter. She looked like a toy next to the massive hull of the ship.

They threw us a few more lines, and we managed to hook them around the cleats and the remaining winches. The crew unfurled a rope ladder down the side of the ship. It looked more like a heavy-duty fishing net that swayed between the ship and Sogno. We realized how dangerous this had become, and that our surviving the rescue operation was not a given. I stared in disbelief as I tried to imagine grabbing hold of a section of the mesh ladder amidst the violent pitching of the two vessels.

We had to jump from Sogno to the webbed ladder in 20-foot seas, which meant that at times the height of our sailboat was above the freighter. Each of us had to calculate the height at a given moment and jump to catch the ladder with our hands and feet. Captain Bob was the first to go. He was significantly overweight and had trouble getting ahold of the ladder. But his heft propelled him squarely against it, and he was able to insert his feet into the openings. He carefully climbed up, slowly taking it one step at a time. It was painful to watch him struggle all the way to the top. We breathed a sigh of relief when the crew leaned over the ship's guardrail to pull him up onto the safety of their deck.

David was the next in line, but he again began to panic. He couldn't get himself together. He needed more time. I had wanted to wait with Jim, but it was clear that I should go next. I stared up at the wall of steel before me, and it seemed that everything went silent. I could hear my heart racing in my chest and the blood pulsing at my temples. Jim's admonitions and instructions seemed distant and muffled. I had to make my move, so I took a deep breath and leapt toward the ladder. I felt the coarse rope against the raw skin on my hands and tightened my grip. When I made contact, I could feel the adrenaline race through my body, and I scurried up the webbing as quickly as I could. I was up to the deck before my fear could take hold. The crew hoisted me over the rail, and as I looked back, I was startled to see Sogno being thrown about so many feet below with the net ladder swaying with her.

David was next in line, and there was no time to delay. Although he was still in panic mode when his turn came, he made a frantic leap from Sogno. With his arms flailing, David caught the rope in his hands, but his feet slipped, and he could not seem to insert either of them into the openings. He was dangling by his hands as the waves knocked him and the two vessels up and down. Another wave lifted Sogno up and towards the freighter. It was heading directly to where David's legs were hanging. If he didn't move quickly, the colliding boats would cut them off. Time seemed to stand still as we watched it all occur in slow motion. Just a moment before Sogno hit the ship, David pulled his legs up and onto the ladder. Had he waited any longer, he would have lost his legs and possibly his life.

Having seen this, Jim decided that there was no way he was going to take that chance. We stood back and watched Sogno get lifted above the freighter by 10 or 15 feet and then below by 15 or 20 feet. I could see that he was cooking up some type of scheme, but I was growing more anxious by the second. All I wanted was for him to get off the sailboat and onto the ship. Then it happened. A wave lifted Sogno high above the deck of the ship. Jim leapt off of Sogno and jumped down onto the deck with a tuck and roll. He had made it.

After that, everything seemed to be happening so quickly. Once we were safely on board the rescue ship, the engines were engaged, and the ship began to move slowly forward. Our attention then turned to Sogno and what to do about her. It became clear to the captain that there was no way to lift her out of the ocean and place her on the deck. The only option was to tow her behind the ship. But that is where basic physics came into play. Ships generally steam at about 30-40 knots because their hull length is huge at more than 300 feet, whereas Sogno was only 50 feet in length. The maximum speed that a boat can travel is based upon the length of the hull. If you try to drag a vessel any faster than its hull speed, it will dig into the water and go under. The fastest a 50-foot sailboat can go is approximately nine to ten knots.

Now that the towlines were set and the ship began

to move forward, Sogno was dragged back and forth across the wake of the ship. As the freighter began to steam ahead, Sogno followed steadily until the ship began to pick up speed. You could actually see the bow of the sailboat angling down into the water. By then, the lines began to snap. The line at the stern of the boat caught under the outboard dinghy motor. As the line snapped taught, the motor shot into the air. There was a towline to the bow that was run through the bowsprit to the two front deck cleats. These cleats gave way almost immediately. A second towline had been secured to the starboard side winch in the cockpit. Those winches were the next to go; one by one, they popped off and sailed into the sea. It was as if we were watching Sogno come apart piece by piece. We gaped at the sight in disbelief; no words were exchanged as the scene unfolded before us. Due to the severe seas and the pitching vessels, additional attempts to secure her would be dangerous and life-threatening.

Finally, as the remaining lines broke away, Sogno set adrift into the ocean. She became smaller and smaller against the horizon until we could no longer see her at all. Jim and I turned to each other and exchanged a look of despair. Our dream boat had disappeared.

When it was clear that the towing operation was

a failure, the crew turned its attention to the four of us. We were led to our cabins and shown the location of the facilities. The cabins were seven by eight-foot cells appointed with only the basic necessities; it felt like we had just joined the Navy. Bob and David went to their respective rooms in silence. I was shown to my room but continued to follow as they brought Jim to his. The door closed, and we sat on his bunk and quietly embraced. There were no words that could express the emotions roiling within us. We remained there for a very long time until we laid back to rest.

Soon we were alerted to join the crew for supper. Meals were simple utilitarian events held in a small mess hall. The crew didn't linger to socialize with us or chat with each other; they just ate and returned to their stations. However, the captain and crew of the freighter could not have been more kind and generous to us as they fed us and kept us safe and warm.

The captain and Jim struck up an easy rapport, and Jim was soon invited onto the bridge, where he was able to observe their navigation and daily routine. Each in our own way, we tried to distract ourselves from the emotional storm that was raging within us. Jim pelted the captain with countless questions regarding the ship and how it functioned. True to form, Jim asked for a tour of the engine room, delighting the crew with his interest. I went along simply because I needed the distraction. But I was bored to tears as he continued asking questions and they answered each in agonizing detail.

After a day or so, we discovered that there was little to do on the ship, so Jim asked the captain if he could borrow his computer. He hoped to chronicle our entire experience while it was still fresh in his mind. Day after day, I sat with him on the bridge as we tried to record the previous two weeks of sailing. However useful that exercise was, it caused us both to re-live all that had just happened and only served to emphasize what we had lost. Although we were physically and emotionally exhausted, true rest evaded us as visions of each trauma played over and over in our minds.

During the week or so that it took to get to port, Jim and I had very little contact with Captain Bob or David. They stayed clear of us, clinging to each other like elementary school buddies who had just been bullied. I don't know if they blamed us for all that had happened or if they were simply traumatized. I wanted to reach out to them, but I found that I had nothing to say. I really couldn't comfort them when I was in such need of it myself.

Our idle time on the boat provided a fertile ground for worry and anxiety. We had no idea what to do at that point. We had lost our investment and our dream of a new life of sailing the Caribbean. Neither of us had jobs in St. Thomas because Sogno was going to allow us to start a sailing charter business. The rest of our savings was lost due to the crash of the stock market after 9/11. The practical details of life were pushing to the forefront of our minds even as we were reeling from the perilous rescue we had just experienced. We still had to purchase plane tickets for the four of us to get back to our respective homes. Nothing seemed to make sense, and life certainly did not seem fair at that point.

The ship was heading to Venezuela and would pass right by St. Thomas and Puerto Rico. We hoped that they would be able to pull into the harbor and drop us off, so Jim asked the captain. As accommodating as he was, the captain explained that his only responsibility was to rescue us and bring us safely to land. He agreed to contact the company that contracted the ship to inquire, but he wasn't very hopeful. As he suspected, the shipping company refused to allow another stop to drop us off. The rescue had cost them time and money, and they were anxious to get back on course to complete their mission.

It would be another week before we would get back home to St. Thomas, but we had to land in another country. In our hurry to abandon Sogno, we left behind all of the essential gear that we had packed to bring with us. That included identification, money, and our passports. Without our passports, we would not be able to get through customs.

During my many travel tours with students, I was always concerned that someone would lose a passport. I instructed everyone to make several copies of the photo page, leave one at home, and carry another in a separate place from the original passport. I had followed my own instructions, so I knew there was a solution to our dilemma. I used the satellite phone to call a friend of ours in St. Thomas and asked her to go into our house and fax our passport copies to the U.S. embassy in Venezuela. I hoped that it might speed up our process once we landed.

When the ship neared the port of Caracas, the captain alerted the harbormaster that he had rescued four sailors at sea. When the Venezuelan customs officer discovered that we were undocumented, the ship was not allowed to dock, so the captain anchored a mile or so away. It was nearly six hours before a police boat pulled up to collect us. The four of us boarded the boat and headed into the port. The police precinct looked as if it had been through numerous hurricanes, with rusted bars and crumbling cement. We were unceremoniously placed in jail cells while they contacted the U.S. embassy. This was yet another blow to my already battered psyche; the cells were cramped with odors of stale urine and mold wafting through the air.

We were eventually released and picked up approximately three hours later and brought to the U.S. embassy. We were so grateful and relieved to see them. Since they had our passport copies, it took no time to reissue new ones. They gave us each $500 and directed us to a hotel where we could spend the night. That was the last time we saw Bob and David. We bid them a cordial goodbye and safe return home. We were all able to catch flights home the following day. Our return to St. Thomas was met with great fanfare from our friends who were anxious to hear our harrowing story. It was now December.

CHAPTER
17

Back in our home in St. Thomas, Jim and I decided that we needed to cheer ourselves up. Since our tradition in San Francisco had been to decorate every inch of our home, we went in search of a Christmas tree. It seemed odd to me that they sold beautiful live pine trees on St. Thomas. Each year, there were numerous shipments of them from Canada. So we headed to the shipping container from which they sold the trees and searched for the perfect Christmas tree. Though we had little money, we bought the largest tree we could find.

It was 14 feet tall, the largest tree we had ever had. It

would reach up to the rafters and look majestic in our great room. It would be the first thing people would see when they entered our doors. With that huge tree strapped to the roof of our SUV, we went to the Big K-mart because we didn't own a stand for a tree trunk that large. The selection wasn't great, but we were able to find a plastic stand whose diameter would fit the trunk of our great tree.

Luckily, we could drive right up to the entrance of our house. We opened the two massive front doors, creating a large enough opening for the tree. I quickly went through the doors, cleared the closest corner of the room, and set the tree stand in place. By then, Jim had untied the tree from the roof of the SUV. We hoisted it up on our shoulders and carried it the short distance through the doors. With the stand affixed to the base of the tree, we carefully lifted it to its upright position. It was magnificent in that space.

After we located the moving boxes that held our decorations, we piled them in the great room. Jim carefully unwrapped the beautiful ornaments that he had bought from countries all over the world. Amazingly, not a single one was damaged from the move. That, in and of itself, was a minor miracle. We had to get a ladder to decorate the upper part of the tree and place the angel at the top. The most difficult part was stringing the lights; it took hours. But when we had finished, it was by far the most beautiful Christmas tree we had ever had. Jim put his arms around me and kissed me. Neither of us spoke as we gazed upon our handiwork. Then he turned to me, looked deeply into my eyes and said, "Merry Christmas, my love." At that moment, I knew we would be just fine. We could weather any storm, quite literally, as long as we had each other.

We awoke to a beautiful December day in St. Thomas. The Christmas winds cooling the island blew gently through our open windows while our wild roosters crowed their daily greeting. I opened the bedroom door and began to cross to the kitchen when I saw something glittering in the sunlight. Without my glasses, I couldn't tell what it was, but as I continued to walk, there was more and more light reflecting off the terra-cotta floor. Jim and I turned toward the great room where we discovered that the plastic tree stand had failed. The Christmas tree had fallen during the night, shattering almost all of the glass ornaments we had collected throughout our lives together. We were in shock once again. When he gathered his composure, Jim turned to me and ironically said, "Are there any other things in our lives that we love? We might as well throw them in the trash now."

Though this latest misfortune was not life-threatening, it added one more blow to our already fragile emotional states. We were both numb.

I took out a broom and dustpan, and Jim manned the vacuum cleaner as we began to clean up all the broken glass from the tile floors. Alex, who always managed to be in the center of all our activity, had to be kept out on the lanai so that she would not walk through the hundreds of shards of glass and get cut. She was scratching at the door and barking at us as we swept each inch of the three rooms that were showered with tiny pieces of glass. We then hoisted up the tree with a rope and used wire to tie it to the beams near the ceiling.

We had lost almost all of our beautiful ornaments. To us, they were more than trinkets from different parts of the world. Each one represented a different period in our lives, a vacation together, or a special moment; once decorated, our Christmas tree was a visual representation of our shared history as a couple. It told our story. After the clean-up was complete, I went to our storage room and pulled out the boxes in which we had stored our decorations. Though we had acquired many new and beautiful ornaments over the years, I hadn't been able to discard the old ones that I had started collecting in high school. Many of them were tattered or discolored, so Jim called them our "Christmas Uglies." We hung them on our tree that morning for the first time in many years.

During this time, the close community of friends that we had made during our brief time in St. Thomas was very attentive to us. They brought us food and checked in with us on a regular basis. They would not let us wallow in self-pity. They drew us out for dinner parties and gatherings during the holiday season. We were almost coerced to participate in an annual tradition on St. Thomas called Christmas on Main Street. After the cruise ships leave port and most of the tourists have left, they block traffic from the main thoroughfare, creating a pedestrian zone. All of the stores that normally close by sundown open up for local residents, offering huge discounts to the local holiday shoppers. A festive air permeates the downtown neighborhood of Charlotte Amalie.

A group of us got together for dinner at a great little restaurant that evening before we went off to do our Christmas shopping. By this time, many people on the island knew who we were and what had happened to us on the boat. We were becoming local legends. Before dinner was over, many of our friends surprised us with gifts. As we unwrapped each one, we discovered that they had each bought us an ornament to add to our tree, each with an island theme. We were both overwhelmed and were brought to tears. We may have known these friends for only three short months, but they had quickly become our St. Thomas family and were our greatest supports. We knew that whatever the future held, we would be able to overcome the obstacles that were presently in our way. There was hope that happiness was still within our reach and that these friends would play a major role in bringing that to fruition.

PART II

THE
RECOVERY

CHAPTER
18

After Christmas, Jim secured a job with a local Internet provider, and soon he was back in his routine as a workaholic. He was the first to arrive at the office every morning and the last to leave at the end of the day. His office was directly across from where the cruise ships docked. Hundreds of tourists browsed the many duty-free jewelry and electronics shops every day. We only owned one car, so I drove Jim to work each morning and picked him up late each afternoon. Expecting a tropical paradise, I was shocked by the heavy traffic on the island. There were few main roads, and they were always lined with taxis picking up tourists from the cruise ships and ferrying them to beaches or into Charlotte Amalie. Driving a half-mile could take up to an hour. The stretch of road leading to and from those docks was the busiest and most crowded on the entire island. I was lucky enough to traverse it twice a day.

I was eagerly looking for a position as a choir director or teacher. Although I was feeling burned out during my last years in San Francisco, I was certainly not ready for retirement. My self-image was tightly intertwined with my identity as a conductor and teacher. I longed to get back into the classroom and in front of a choir. Though there was a great need for teachers in St. Thomas, the application process was quite complicated. Funding for public schools was inadequate, and it took months to get a teaching position approved. In addition, the school year was already halfway over. I needed to look for other options until the next academic year began the following September.

Because of my work as Director of Publications at the high school in San Francisco, I was able to get an interview for a copywriter position in the communications department at the University of the Virgin Islands. I made sure to bring copies of the quarterly magazines that I had published the previous year and was confident that I would get the job. They were impressed with the quality of my work, and I was excited at the prospect of a new job. I had a good feeling about the job; it just felt right for me. However, weeks went by with no word from the university. I finally made a follow-up phone call and discovered that the position had gone to someone else. One of our friends explained that it was very rare for a new resident to get a job that wasn't in retail. Many people move to the island expecting paradise, then leave within the first year when they discover that island life is more complicated and difficult than they had anticipated. I was told by a number of locals that I would have to be there for a while to prove that I was committed to being a true resident of St. Thomas. I was assured, after that, they would scoop me up.

Though I was very disappointed, I was able to get a part-time position using my desktop publishing skills at an advertising agency directly next door to Jim's office. I was hoping to find some stimulation and human interaction to get me out of my solitary days at home. Unfortunately, it was free-lance work, which meant that I had to work from home in the sweltering heat. Because of the high cost of electricity, we did not have air conditioning in our house. We had assumed that refreshing tropical breezes would keep us cool throughout the year. However, the soaring temperatures and high humidity had me sweating at my desk. I regularly took walks to the lanai to take in our gorgeous view and grab something cold to drink before heading back to my sweaty station.

After finishing my work project each day, I looked forward to getting in the air-conditioned car; I put the air on max and positioned the vents directly at my face. Often times, I would drive to the K-Mart and wander the aisles aimlessly in order to cool off. Jim, on the other hand, dressed in wool pants and long sleeve shirts. His office was so cold that he would often go outdoors on his breaks just to warm up. Our conversations after his return from work would often be like this:

"How was your day, Mario?"

"It was fine. But it was brutally hot and humid."

"It doesn't feel that bad now."

"Are you kidding? It's like a sauna out here."

"Maybe you just have to adjust to it. You'll get used to it."

"Yeah, and how about those mosquitoes? Will I get used to those too?"

He could not dissuade me from my misery.

Sitting at my desk each day, swarms of mosquitoes would attack my legs. The room seemed to be infested. But however much they tortured me, Jim suffered many times more. He was a virtual mosquito magnet. I was grateful when he got home because they would finally leave me alone and attack him. It was so bad that we bought a contraption that looked like a mini tennis racket. It was battery operated and put out an electric pulse when prompted. I recall simply gliding it around the back of his head and down his back to the satisfying sound of crackling pops of dead mosquitoes foiled in their attempts to draw his blood. Despite the heat and humidity, he gave up wearing shorts and tee shirts. He wanted as much of his body covered as possible for protection from those voracious insects.

Mosquitoes notwithstanding, we had settled into a comfortable rhythm and were slowly getting used to our new reality. Jim was a military brat whose father was an officer in the Army. His family moved frequently when he was a child. Jim and his two brothers were accustomed to beginning the school year in new schools and making new friends. He quickly learned to adapt to the many new towns or cities in which they lived. He made the best of each situation because he knew that it wouldn't last forever, and he believed that there was something to learn in each place. He loved meeting new people and could strike up a conversation with anyone. There were many occasions when I would be standing beside him, impatiently waiting to leave, while he became best friends with a sales clerk at the local grocery store.

Since I didn't have a full-time job, I spent most of my day alone creating advertisements on my desktop computer in our home office. Our cisterns were located directly below the office and our bedroom. You could simply lift a two-foot square panel off the tile floor to see the hundreds of gallons of rainwater that were collected from our roof. There was no city water on most of the island, so this was how most of us got our supply. Unfortunately, still water is a fertile breeding ground for the beloved mosquito. Our home office was overrun with them. The office was on the south side of the house and was exposed to the glaring sun for most of the day; it was the hottest room in the house. The heat and humidity were so draining that, by the time Jim got home, I was like a wet dishrag.

My lonely days and lack of purpose weighed heavily on me, and I became increasingly despairing. I needed to be with other people. Many days, after finishing my advertising work, I would hop into the car and drive to visit my friend Claire who worked at a spiritual shop in Redhook. In addition to inspirational books, the shop sold crystals, incense, and fairy dust. Jim began to call her Clairy Fairy and playfully mocked us both when we got into our deep spiritual conversations. She was the most positive person I have ever met, filled with goodwill and energy; it exuded from her very core. Claire had a great sense of humor, and we laughed a lot. We had met shortly after we got to St. Thomas.

I was trying to get connected with the music scene on the island, so I sought out every little performance I could find. One evening we went to Redhook to hear several local singers. Chairs were set up on the outdoor deck of the harbor house, and the stage consisted of one single riser with a few amplifiers, a microphone, and a keyboard. The singer was entirely at home as she began her set. She had this sensual alto voice that poured from her lips like syrup. Her blue eyes sparkled, and her smile electrified the audience. I had to meet her, so after she finished singing, I zipped right over to her.

"Hi, I'm Mario, and this is Jim. We just moved to the island."

"Welcome to St. Thomas! My name is Claire."

"I just have to tell you that you were wonderful. Your voice is just stunning!"

"Oh, I don't know about that, but I'm glad you came. It was a pretty thin crowd tonight."

"No, Claire, I am serious. I've been a voice teacher for years, and I've heard so many singers. You really have something special."

"Oh, well then, I can tell that we are going to be best friends forever!"

Claire was my lifeline. Whenever I felt lonely, I drove to the store and just hung out with her during her shift. We chatted about our lives and tried to make sense of our respective journeys. Then we would delve into the meaning of the various crystals in the shop and all that psychic mumbo jumbo, as Jim had affectionately named it. She and I connected on a deeper level, and we were truly grateful to be in each other's lives.

Despite my musical hobbies and budding friendships, my depression worsened. It began insidiously, such that I hardly noticed it. I didn't seem to have motivation for any of the projects on my list. I didn't want to get out of bed in the morning, and I was always tired. I began to take naps just to numb to pain. The beauty of the island was completely lost on me; taking the opportunity to swim or go snorkeling held no allure. I just wanted to escape. Images of San Francisco filled my mind, and I longed to have our old lives back. As the weeks passed, it worsened, and I sank into a very dark depression. Jim and I would be walking along the harbor when he would look at me and see my despair. "Mario, stay out of the hole," he would say. Or, because my Dad had always been a pessimist, Jim would try to make me laugh by calling me by my father's name. "Larry, what are you thinking about? Come back to me, Larry." I tried as hard as I could to remain positive, but it eluded me.

My days were framed by driving Jim to and from work. The routine just reinforced the hopelessness that I felt. In order to get to his office near the cruise ship docks, I would sit in bumper-to-bumper traffic for an hour or more. I had to lower the windows and turn off the air conditioning so that I wouldn't overheat the engine. I was miserable.

Four months after our initial boat trauma, I was on my way to pick up Jim. Quite unexpectedly, I received a call from the Bahamian Coast Guard informing us that Sogno was spotted about 90 miles east of Nassau. That was the kick that I needed. I believed that we could recover the boat and salvage as much as possible from what was left. When Jim got into the car, I began babbling so that he could barely understand what I was talking about.

"Slow down, Mario. What did they say, exactly? Did they indicate what condition the boat was in?"

"No, I didn't think to ask, but if they spotted her, she's obviously still afloat. We can salvage quite a bit, don't you think?"

"Look, Mario, I am sure that by now, someone has stripped her clean of anything valuable."

"You don't know that for sure, Jim. Don't you think it's worth a look?"

"Yeah, I don't know. Do you really want to go out there in the open ocean again? Let's just cut our losses."

"But, Jim, it's just 90 miles offshore. We would be close to land, and we could ask our friends there to help us."

"Let's just slow down and think this through. This would be incredibly costly, and we don't have the cash right now."

"But Jim, if we recover the boat, those expenses would be covered."

"That's a big IF, Mario. After what we experienced in November, I am not keen on putting our lives in danger again."

Jim was totally against going. After our traumatic rescue, he was not willing to place his life at risk again. He also realized how perilous this adventure could be, and our brush with death was still fresh in his mind. Images of the 40-foot wall of steel barreling down upon the sailboat during the rescue flashed into his mind. The mast slamming against the hull of the ship and piercing into the cabin of Sogno was still a vivid memory.

But I was aching with the pain and anger of having our dreams ripped from our grasp. There was an injustice that needed to be made right; we had lost most of our savings, which represented years of hard work as well as the security for our future. Our sense of adventure, which had always propelled us forward into exciting new life experiences, was extinguished. In its place was fear and insecurity. We had no drive or desire to take any risks, even those that were seemingly ordinary. The entire plan to move to the islands was to live our dream retirement on a beautiful sailboat. Instead, we were left with no jobs, no money, and no boat in the heat and humidity of St. Thomas. I was not about to let go so easily. Jim said that I was like a little terrier growling and biting at the pant leg of anyone who caused us harm; that I wouldn't let go until I got my way. I knew that we had done nothing wrong, that somehow justice would prevail and we would be made whole – both financially and emotionally. I was determined to recapture our dream.

I had to convince Jim of the necessity of going after the boat. We were still parked outside his office, looking out at the cruise ships slowly leaving port.

"If we don't try to recover the boat, then we will have lost everything. What was the point of this entire struggle? What did this whole nightmare mean?"

"Yeah, I'm not so sure. Perhaps there is no deeper meaning, Mario. We barely escaped our last voyage with our lives."

"After four months at sea, they spotted Sogno. That has to be a sign. We can't just give up!" I replied.

"There you go again with your supernatural hocus pocus, Mario!"

Reluctantly, Jim relented. He was angry as well, but his anger was tempered by the reality of the dangers involved with a salvage attempt. With little income from our jobs, we were running out of money; our savings were nearly depleted. Given that a major portion of our savings was used to buy the boat and move to St. Thomas, we needed to take care of the recovery as cheaply as possible. Salvage companies charge exorbitant fees and usually ravage any boat they recover by stripping off all the valuable electronics and equipment. Strangely, that is completely legal in maritime law. Our only option was to do all of it by ourselves. So, with our limited funds, we decided to move forward to recover our sailboat and our dream.

During the first two months on St. Thomas, before we had taken possession of Sogno, we met a wonderful guy from Nassau. Jean Pierre worked with at-risk youth, teaching them how to sail and giving them essential life skills beyond their boating experience. Having been a teacher, I had a great deal of respect for his work and his mission. He hoped that we would be willing to work with him so that he could expand his program to St. Thomas. Just like so many others who had heard of our sailing mishap, he was in disbelief. When we called him in Nassau, he was enthusiastically willing to help us. He had many local friends in the Coast Guard and the sailing industry. He said that he would try to get more accurate information regarding the coordinates of Sogno and would begin to make inquiries as to the best way to recover the boat.

Mom and Dad had come to stay us in St. Thomas during the cold Connecticut winter, so we asked our friends to check in on them while we were away. We told them of our plan and assured them that we would be back within the week. We tried, unsuccessfully, to put their minds at ease. They had never liked the idea of our first sailing expedition. After hearing about everything that went wrong in November, they were quite worried about our safety. With his strong Italian accent, Dad was quite fierce in expressing his disdain for this hair-brained idea.

"What? Are you crazy? How are you going to get all the way out into the ocean to find the boat?"

"Dad, we are friends with the Coast Guard," I exaggerated. "They can pinpoint its location with pretty good accuracy."

"What happens if you get stuck in another storm or hurricane? You could drown!"

"Don't worry so much, Dad! We know what we're doing. We are going to be just fine."

When departure time arrived, they put on brave faces and bid us safe travels as we embarked upon our next seafaring adventure. I kissed them both, and Mom's embrace was particularly tight. I knew she was frightened.

CHAPTER 19

We arrived in Nassau on Thursday, April 4th, and got settled at Jean Pierre's small apartment. With his connections, we met with the Coast Guard the following day to calculate the boat's location based upon the weather conditions and currents. Jean Pierre suggested that the quickest way to get out to Sogno was to rent a seaplane. Both Jim and I hesitated when we heard how costly it was going to be, but we acquiesced. We just wanted to get this done and resolved as quickly as possible.

Later that day, we boarded the seaplane with a great deal of confidence and excitement. But as soon as we took off, the pilot quashed our high hopes. He said that it would be difficult to locate our boat even with the accurate coordinates from the Coast Guard. It was like looking for a needle in a haystack. As we scanned the waters out of the windows, all we saw were miles and miles of ocean with little white caps upon each wave. It seemed that the pilot was right; it was a tremendously vast ocean, and our boat was just a tiny speck. As we reached the location of our coordinates, the pilot began a systematic sweep of the area in a grid pattern. Time passed, and it seemed as if we would not have any luck finding Sogno. The pilot told us that we could continue for another 20 minutes or so before we would have to head back.

The four of us sat in silence, desperate to see something. Then, out of nowhere, it appeared. A little white dot grew larger as it bobbed up and down in the sea below us. We were all in disbelief. The plane slowly descended and circled the boat. The companionway entrance was wide open, letting four months of rain and waves pour into the cabin. Despite that fact, it looked as if the boat was still in pretty good shape. We were anxious to land the plane, board our sailboat, and figure out our next step. As we flew near the surface of the water, we realized that there was a good deal of wind and a significant chop on the water. The pilot tried to land, but after several attempts, he informed us that it would not be safe. We had brought all the equipment needed for the recovery effort, and we were ready to go. We tried to persuade him, but he would not relent. I feared that our luck in finding Sogno would not hold if we had to make a second attempt. Despite our desperate pleas, the pilot would not give in. We made our way back to Nassau, leaving Sogno afloat in the distance behind us.

We were all deflated and felt our hopes of recovery begin to wane. We were keenly aware of the fact that we had just wasted thousands of dollars on the rental of the seaplane and that we were no closer to getting our boat back. At this point, Jean Pierre was determined to make this all work, even more so than either Jim or me. His positive attitude and drive persuaded us not to give up hope. He suggested that we hire a motorboat to bring us out and possibly tow the sailboat back with us. Through his many connections, Jean Pierre was able to persuade a friend to rent us a twin-engine, 20-foot pontoon boat. We could motor out to Sogno the next day. We had a new plan in place, and we both felt that we were in good hands with Jean Pierre. He had many years of sailing experience and put us at ease. He was quite confident that we would recover the boat and that we'd be sailing together in short order.

That night, we slept on the couch in Jean Pierre's apartment. I had trouble falling asleep; it was a very restless night. I kept picturing the boat in my mind after seeing her from the seaplane earlier that day. I had a dream that I motored out to Sogno on my own. Alone, I boarded the boat and took in the heartbreaking scene and was shocked to see all the damage. Strangely, I was not upset. I felt emotionally detached, simply observing all that was around me; I was just glad to have the boat back. I walked down the steps to the main cabin and saw a man sitting at the table with his head bowed down. He lifted his head to greet me and, although there were no facial details, he seemed familiar. In an even, emotionless voice, he said, "I've been waiting for you." At that moment, I felt an overwhelming sense of despair. My shoulders drooped, and my head hung low. I had a paralyzing sense of helplessness and grief; it felt as if someone very dear to me had just died. At that moment, I woke up with a start, and I couldn't shake that heavy feeling for the rest of the night.

Saturday morning was busy with preparations. Since we didn't have our own tools, we had to buy whatever we might need to repair the boat. We were racking up the charges on our credit card, but at least we would be able to get our boat back and recover some of our losses. We went to a lumberyard to buy some plywood and two by fours in order to build a wooden rudder. We found a used outboard motor with an extended shaft that would likely work if we mounted it on the stern of the boat. We hoped that using the outboard motor would allow us to propel Sogno under her own power, or at least to help move her great mass while being towed. We weren't sure how long our recovery effort would take, so we got supplies for a three-day stay on the sailboat. We made sure to get water and food that would not take any preparation and was easy to consume. During all these chores, we felt productive and confident in our eventual success.

Sogno was about 90 miles from shore, and we knew it would be a rough ride motoring all that way in the pontoon boat. Even with the twin 200 horsepower engines, it took us nearly seven hours to get out there. As expected, the chop of the sea was intense. The pounding of the boat on every wave beat us to hell, and the surf crashed over the bow, soaking us thoroughly. We were pounded as we were thrown up and down as we hit each wave. Between the beating of the boat and the spray of the surf, we were wet, sore, and uncomfortable within an hour. But we focused on our ultimate goal of salvaging Sogno. There were still several hours to go before we would be in range of the coordinates given to us by the Coast Guard.

It was a brutal journey. After a brief stop in Spanish Wells for fuel and a bite to eat, we were off again. As we neared the range of the coordinates from the previous day, we recalled the words of the pilot when he said that it would be like finding a needle in a haystack. Without the perspective of flying above the sea, it was proving to be more challenging to find our boat. In addition, we had to estimate the new location-based upon its drift from the currents during the last 24 hours. However, there was no need to doubt our calculations – just an hour later, we spotted her bobbing calmly in the rolling seas. It was almost eerie how easily we found her given the vastness of the ocean. But there she was, almost beckoning us to come aboard. We saw that the mast was missing, but other than that, she looked to be in good condition.

Strangely, we spotted Sogno only three miles from the coordinates that the Coast Guard had calculated. Finding the boat in that immense stretch of sea was improbable enough, but seeing her two days in a row with relative ease was unimaginable. We were so excited. As we motored closer to the boat, it seemed as if we were in an aquarium. There were hundreds of fish swimming near the surface; they were feeding off of the algae growing on the hull of the boat. The multi-colored fish caught the sunlight as they swam in the turquoise waters. There were fish that were bright yellow and black, silver and blue, parrotfish, angelfish, and many others. It was beautiful. But when we boarded the boat, we found that she was covered with scores of dead flying fish; the stench was awful. Sogno didn't look as good upon closer inspection. There was a mass of mangled rope, cable, and sharp metal on the bow of the boat from its fateful encounter with the freighter. Once onboard, we could see that she was leaning down toward the bow as she had obviously taken on a considerable amount of water.

Descending the stairs into the main cabin, we discovered that it had about three to four feet of water sloshing to and fro as the boat bobbed in the waves. The once-luxurious leather seat cushions had detached and were floating alongside the floorboards that had come loose. Articles from many of the cabinets that had broken open were scattered in the sludge that coated the floor. The water was slimy, and there was the stench of sewage as well as rotting wood and mold. The odor was overwhelming, and we had to go above to breathe some fresh air before inspecting the rest of our equipment.

Once our stomachs had settled, we went down below again. The engine compartment was directly below the companionway steps. Jim lifted the steps to gain access in order to get a read on its condition. We had hoped that we would be able to start the engine after some minor adjustments. But the reality was that it had been submerged in saltwater for four months. Jim tinkered with it for a while until he resigned himself to the fact that it was impossible. After having seen Sogno from the seaplane the day before, we thought she would be in pretty good shape.

But she was in much worse condition than we had imagined. Our perspective from the plane gave us the illusion that it would only take some minor fixes to get her going again. Even the ever-optimistic Jean Pierre felt more than a little disappointed and discouraged as we continued to assess the damage.

Since the boat had lost its mast and rudder, there was nothing to steady her in the water. She bobbed up and down and side to side with each passing wave. All three of us found it impossible to keep our stomachs still. Each of us began to feel queasy as soon as we boarded Sogno and tried to limit our time in the cabin below to stave off the seasickness.

Throughout the process of recovering the boat, I continued to feel a dark energy surrounding Sogno. It seemed that she had confiscated our personal items, objects that were dear to us, and would not release them. She seemed to have a life of her own. Each time I went below to search for something that I had left there four months ago, I would get violently ill. I would press on and search each cabinet, then rush up on deck to puke. The memory of my nightmare the night before stuck with me. I began to get spooked. The sound of hundreds of gallons of water sloshing from side to side within the cabin was chilling.

Up on deck, Jean Pierre prepared to dive under the boat to inspect the hull and the rudder. He jumped into the water without a splash. Once below, he cut away the sails that were tangled in the lines of the mast that had been snapped off during the rescue back in November. We used to call Jean Pierre "fish-boy" because he swam like a mermaid. He was incredibly fast and agile under the water; he looked like he had fins propelling him forward. So when he frantically popped up out of the water in a panic, we knew something was wrong. He could not stay below for long because he spotted a number of sharks feeding off of our beautiful aquarium. They were feasting upon the many fish swimming around the boat. After he spotted the sharks, he jumped up out of the water and quickly got on board. They were black sharks, which are quite dangerous and not friendly to humans invading their feeding grounds. It was obviously unsafe to go into the water around Sogno. But after his inspection, he reported that the bottom of the boat was in perfect condition. We were elated because we knew that we would definitely be able to repair her once we got her into a boatyard.

Our next step was to get the hundreds of gallons of water out of the cabin. We had to empty as much as possible before we could attempt any of our other solutions. Towing or using the outboard motor would not be effective with so much extra weight dragging Sogno down. So we began a bucket brigade and started emptying the water from the cabin. After a few hours of bailing water, we decide to give the wooden rudder and outboard motor a try. We tried to mount them on the stern of Sogno but found we had underestimated the length required for the propeller and rudder to reach the water. The extended propeller was approximately five feet long; when we tried to attach it to the boat's stern, we discovered that it barely touched the surface.

The wooden rudder was about eight feet in length, and even that was not long enough to reach into the water.

We decided that we would continue bailing water in order to lighten the weight enough to tow her in without the rudder. By nightfall, our arms were sore from bailing, but we were comforted by the fact that we had made good progress. We decided that we would get a fresh start in the morning and try to tow her at daybreak. We all needed to rest. Due to Jim's meticulous departure preparations back in November, the deck cushions were stored below in the back cabins, and amazingly enough, had remained dry. We brought them up along with some dry blankets and curled up on deck to get some sleep.

CHAPTER 20

During the night, the winds kicked up, and we were tossed about like a beach ball. They blew more vigorously, and the temperature dropped; we could feel the chill against our wet clothing as the wind penetrated the blankets. It had begun to rain, and the wind and waves began to intensify. The spray from the swells became more frequent, and we knew that we had to go below; otherwise, we would be soaked through to the bone. The odor of the foul water was horrific and gave us pause as our stomachs started churning once again. Each of us had already vomited several times that afternoon and did not relish the thought of repeating it. Sogno was listing towards the bow, so we tried to find a dry corner in the stern cabins of the boat where we could warm up. Our time in the back cabin didn't last long.

Jean Pierre was restless, almost manic. He insisted on bailing more water. Around 1:30 a.m., Jean Pierre was out on the deck when he noticed that the 15-foot waves and wind were causing the pontoon boat to slap up against the bow of Sogno. He decided to pull it in and inspect it. The sharp metal stanchions of Sogno had been ripped apart during the rescue in November and hung off the sides of the boat. Jean Pierre discovered that they had punctured one of the inflatable pontoons. He immediately became agitated; this was his friend's boat, and he had reluctantly agreed to rent it to us. Now it was damaged. To add to his concern, it was our only mode of transportation back to Nassau. Jean Pierre yelled to wake us. We joined him on deck to see what the problem was.

"Jim, there is a huge gash on the inflatable. Do we have anything to fix it with?"

"Let me look below. I know we had a patch kit somewhere."

Jim went below, and luckily he found it immediately. He pulled out the largest patch and the rubber glue and boarded the pontoon boat. But with the steady rain and blowing wind, he was having trouble keeping it within his grasp. Jim was frustrated.

"I just can't keep it steady. The spray and rain are making it impossible to keep it dry for the patch."

"You have to fix it! There's no other choice."

"Do you want to give it a try, Jean Pierre? Because I just can't get it to stick."

"No, you know what to do better than me. Keep trying."

Try after try–it became clear that Jim would not be able to repair it. Jean Pierre's anxiety continued to increase, and he decided that he had to stay on the pontoon boat to keep it away from Sogno. It was the only way to prevent further damage.

"You can't stay out there all night, Jean Pierre. What will that do?" Jim asked.

Angrily, he responded, "I have to keep it away from the sailboat. Do you want it to get more damaged?"

"OK, OK. Mario and I are going below to get some sleep. Just call us if you need anything."

Then he shouted at us, "You should be working, not resting! I told you that we needed to tie bumpers to the boat, but you were too tired! Now, look at what's happened."

It wasn't that we were too tired to tie the bumpers on Sogno. With the seas getting rougher, it was too dangerous to walk on deck to tie them on. Given that there was nothing to hold on to while the boat was being tossed about, it was perilous. But with Jean Pierre's anxiety mounting, he was lashing out at both of us. There was no use trying to reason with him. We had to take care of ourselves so that we could be of some use come daybreak.

We tried to settle in the back corner of the stern cabin again, but neither of us could get any more sleep. We gave up and came back up on deck. I am not sure how many hours passed, but as the weather worsened, we realized that the conditions were getting dangerous. Our fatigue was showing, and tensions were running high. After a brief discussion, we decided that we should try to tow Sogno in right then, rather than wait until morning.

We tied the towlines to the pontoon boat and wrapped them around the winches of Sogno. Jean Pierre gave it all he had, revving the engine to full throttle. But even though they were twin 200 horsepower engines, Sogno would not budge. After several more attempts, Jim and I got on the inflatable with Jean Pierre, hoping that the extra weight would help. He then gave it another try; once again, he revved the engines at full throttle. The lines tightened, and the inflatable began to move forward ever so slightly. I held my breath, thinking, "It's working. We're going to be able to tow her in." But then it bounced back again. Jean Pierre tried several more times with no success.

It was nearly impossible to maneuver all of this in the dark, especially with such high seas, but we were determined. We just kept at it, revving the engines time and again, but Sogno wouldn't budge. The inflatable did not have enough mass to tow a 50-foot sailboat. After hours of trying with the outboard and the tow, we decided to wait until dawn so that we would be safer. We hoped that bailing more water from the cabin would lighten it enough for the tow to work. Jean Pierre insisted upon staying on the inflatable until sunrise. Jim tried to reason with him once again, but he wouldn't give in. He felt that he would be better able to safeguard it from bouncing against Sogno if he was on board.

"If I stay on it with the engines running, I can steer it away when it gets too close to Sogno."

"Jean Pierre, it's still raining, you're going to be freezing by sunrise. At least come in for a little while to warm up," I encouraged him.

"I can't risk it getting more damaged. I'm going to

have enough trouble explaining this to my buddy in Nassau. He's going to be pissed."

He had promised his friend that he would be careful with the boat, and this was going to be no minor fix.

The wind blew harder, and the waves knocked Sogno in every direction. The rain became sporadic, but with every gust, we got soaked once again. Jean Pierre finally decided to join us on Sogno after he was so wet and cold that he could no longer stand it.

We needed to get some rest; otherwise, we would be worthless in the morning. So we decided that we would take shifts on deck. If any ships passed by, we would try to signal them. Jim took the first shift while Jean Pierre went below to get warm. We were all utterly soaked from the rain and the spray from the waves crashing over the boat. Each puff of wind chilled us to the bone. I went below to find some dry blankets, but there were none. Those that we had brought up earlier in the evening were soaked from the rain. Instead, I brought up a box of plastic garbage bags that I had found.

"Here, Jim, rip these open and wrap them around you. At least they will keep you dry and block the wind."

"Great idea, Mario. We need something to prevent us from hypothermia."

Jim was seated on the deck seats, and I was on the floor, trying to stay out of the wind. I wrapped the garbage bags around my legs and covered myself as best I could. The plastic broke the wind and seemed to keep us both dry and warm. But whenever a big gust would blow, the bags would lift and let the breeze through; it felt like an ice-cold tongue licking our shivering bodies. The bags were flapping furiously from the heavy winds. If we moved the wrong way, they would loosen and fill with air. Being exposed to the raw wind made it even more difficult to get warm. After an hour or so, Jim asked me to take over. He was exhausted and needed to close his eyes. But our muscles were sore from hours of bailing water, so just switching positions was agony.

An hour or so later, I spotted a ship. It looked like a cruise line, but I couldn't be sure. We hoped that they would be able to call for help and get us towed into shore. The hand-held radio that we had brought with us wasn't working. It had gotten wet from both rain and seawater, so I used a flashlight to signal the passing ship. Pointing it directly at the bridge, I flicked the light on and off a number of times. The ship's searchlights came on, so I assumed that it had seen our distress signal. I woke Jim, and we continued to flash an SOS beacon. The cruise ship seemed to be coming our way.

I was not sure what would happen or what I was hoping they would do if they spotted us. Perhaps they would call the Coast Guard or even pull us up onto the ship. The idea of getting picked up by a ship of that size was daunting. Images of our harrowing experience on the freighter in November flashed in my mind. But after 15 minutes or so of signaling, the ship turned from us and continued on its way. I don't know if they ever saw us. I can't imagine that they would simply ignore an SOS signal, but who knows. I just could not believe that there was no way for us to contact help, no radio, nor a cell phone. Once again, we were helpless, and the darkness of the night only heightened my fear.

After spotting the cruise ship, we realized that we must have drifted into the shipping lanes and that we were in grave danger. Without any lights or means of communication, we were sitting ducks. The fact that the cruise ship did not spot us was not a good sign. Ships steaming at full speed could easily hit us. I continued my signals in vain as the ship passed us by, hoping that they would see us and turn back. But it merely sailed on until we could no longer see it. It was clear that we needed to remain alert should we be in direct line of any other ships that might come by through the rest of the night.

CHAPTER 21

On Sunday morning, the seas were still very high, and the winds were strong. We later learned that the winds were recorded at 30 to 35 knots. It was about 5 a.m., and we had to make a decision. Jean Pierre was on deck with us when he finally conceded that we were out of options. We set off the EPIRB (Emergency Position-Indicating Radio Beacon,) an SOS signal that alerts the Coast Guard. We didn't know that when the signal reaches the authorities, they immediately call the emergency contact numbers listed in order to confirm that there is an actual emergency. The first number on the list was Jim's Dad in Texas; the Coast Guard called him and asked, "May I speak to Colonel Alexander?

Sir, this is the Bahamian Coast Guard. Do you have a son named James Alexander?"

"Well, yes, that's my son. What's this all about?"

"We just received an SOS signal from the boat he was sailing. Do you where he is located?"

He had no idea that we were out at sea trying to salvage our boat, so he responded, "Jim should be home in St. Thomas. He abandoned that boat back in November. The signal must have gone off on its own. I am sure he's alright."

"Have you spoken to him recently, sir?"

"No, not in a couple of weeks."

"Thank you for your help, Colonel Alexander."

Jim's Dad hung up the phone, believing that we were safe and sound. He told his wife to remind him to call Jim the following day.

Since the Colonel had indicated that we were at home, the Coast Guard found our number on the contact list and called our home in St. Thomas. Mom, already anxious about the recovery expedition, picked up the call from the Coast Guard.

"Good Morning, this is the Bahamian Coast Guard. May we speak to James Alexander or Mario Dell'Olio?"

"Neither of them is here right now. Who did you say

was calling?" Mom asked.

"This is the Coast Guard. Do you know where they are, Ma'am?"

"Jim and my son went to get their boat."

"Where did they go, Ma'am?"

"I'm sorry, but I don't know exactly where. Someone called to say that they had found it. Mario and Jim went to get it back."

"When did they leave?"

"They left here on Thursday, about three days ago."

"Have you heard from them since they left?"

"No, we haven't. Are they OK?"

"We received an emergency signal from the boat, and we just needed to check on that. I am sure that there is nothing to worry about. We will continue to investigate. Thank you."

That confirmed that the SOS was indeed real, and that set the rescue mission in motion.

Mom and Dad were alone at our home in St. Thomas, not knowing what to do or who to contact. Mom stared out the window to the gray waters of the Atlantic Ocean. There was a storm passing through the Virgin Islands, and she pictured Jim and me on a boat in the midst of it. She pulled out her rosary beads and began to pray. Dad paced back and forth on the lanai, bemoaning the fact that we had ever left our comfortable lives in San Francisco.

"These kids! What are they, crazy? They had that beautiful home in San Francisco. Now they live in the jungle."

He never took to the rustic nature of island life. His lament about our predicament continued for 20 minutes or so when he turned to Mom. "Are they going to call us back?" he asked apprehensively.

"I don't know, Larry, they didn't say. I hope so."

At that point, Mom decided that she needed to do something other than worry. We had given them a contact list of people to call if they needed anything. She eventually called our friend Maria who came to the house to stay with them. She assured them that all would be well and that there was no use in worrying. Strangely, she was the most unlikely person to calm my Mom and Dad. She hated everything about boats and sailing. We couldn't get her on a boat if we tried. But Maria is an Italian woman from Staten Island in New York, so she and mom had a lot in common. She was very good at distracting them and, if all else failed, she knew that they could talk about food.

Back on Sogno, we could see land in the distance; just one day earlier, we were 90 miles from the shore. We had drifted significantly during the storm. Jean Pierre decided that he should head into the nearest port to summon help. He tried to persuade me to accompany him, but I felt safer on the sailboat. Ultimately, I did not want to be separated from Jim. Alone and without power or any means of communication, he would have been helpless on Sogno. Two people were necessary to handle any crisis that might occur. I was confident that the Coast Guard would arrive shortly, and I needed to be with Jim. We gave Jean Pierre our credit card with instructions to do what he could once he got to the harbor.

"Do whatever it takes to get someone out here," Jim told him.

"I will. Don't worry. I will get someone to tow you in," he assured us. Handing him the hand-held GPS, Jim said, "Here, take this, you'll need it to find the harbor."

"Got it. Stay safe. Are you sure you want to stay, Mario?"

"Yes, I'm certain, Jean Pierre. Thanks."

"OK. See you soon."

Later, Jean Pierre told us that he had gone to a number

of tow and rescue companies, but no one was willing to go out in the weather conditions. In desperation, he offered someone ten thousand dollars, but there were no takers. He felt helpless and was very worried about our safety. Nothing like this had ever happened to him in all his years of sailing.

After watching Jean Pierre and the pontoon boat fade into the distance, we went below. Jim and I were holed up in the one dry corner of the crew cabin, trying to get warm. We had not slept at all throughout the night and were both physically and emotionally exhausted. We were anxiously awaiting the Coast Guard and figured that we could run up on deck when we heard the roar of the helicopter blades. But at that moment, all we could hear was the wind howling through the cracks in the hull and the waves hitting us from every side. As we drifted in and out of sleep, we both heard unfamiliar noises; they were almost like whispers. It sounded as if there were people whispering out in the main cabin or on deck. Jim asked me if I heard them too. It was eerie, but we knew that because of our physical and emotional exhaustion, our minds were playing tricks on us.

It seemed that time was passing very slowly. Our clothes were soaked, and our flesh was cold. We clung to each other in order to preserve body heat. Each time the boat would rock, or the wind would whistle through the cabin, we shivered anew. Jim's feet felt like cold dead flesh against mine. No matter what we did, we just couldn't seem to warm up.

I turned to look at him at one point. His eyes were wide open. They were glassy and red; he was staring up at the ceiling. I don't know if he was praying, crying, or simply coming to terms with our seemingly hopeless situation. But it was clear that he was struggling, almost as if he was saying goodbye to life during the final moments of quiet. When he noticed me looking at him, he just said, "I love you." A chilling fear ran up my spine. I had never seen such desperation in his eyes. At that moment, we both knew that our survival was tenuous. We had to come to terms with that fact and needed to move forward as best we could.

CHAPTER 22

Did you hear that?" I asked.

"Hear what?"

"I thought I heard an engine."

"You're imagining things, Mario."

"No, I'm certain. I heard a plane or helicopter."

I ran up on deck to signal whoever had come by, but there was no plane or boat in sight. I thought that perhaps I had dreamt it. When I returned to the cabin, Jim said, "Look, Mario, if we don't make contact with the Coast Guard by 2 or 3 p.m., we need to get off this boat."

"Are you kidding me? You mean that we have to abandon her again?"

I looked at him in disbelief. Those waves were about 20-feet high. Dinghies don't fare well in such high seas and are often flipped over. There was no way I was getting into that little boat. We were restless, and it seemed that sleep was not in the cards. An hour or so passed when Jim looked out the porthole window and saw that land was much closer than we had anticipated. There is an extensive reef along the island of Eleuthera called the "Devil's Backbone," and it was much too close for our safety. If we crashed onto the reef, there was no telling how badly we might be injured. He turned to me and firmly said, "We have to get off the boat, NOW!"

I flinched at his tone; the gravity of the command was not lost on me. We got ourselves together, and Jim went to look at the dinghy that he had tied to the bow of the boat. We knew that the only way off of Sogno at this point was on the dinghy. The fact that it was still strapped to the bow was a miracle. It seemed almost inevitable that someone had been on the boat before us, and we were surprised that they didn't take it along with some of the other items that we found missing.

But there was a problem. There was a tangle of lines and metal stanchions all over the dinghy. It was not going to be an easy task to get it loose without puncturing it. This was one of the most frightening moments thus far. With Sogno tossing in the 20-foot waves, Jim went onto the bow to untie the dinghy. He looked like Spiderman as he crawled his way there on his belly with his arms and legs stretched out in order to keep himself balanced. It had been bad enough watching him untangle the sail back in November, clinging to the guide wires with the battering wind and rain. But at least then he was tethered to the boat and wore a life jacket. Now there was nothing left to which he could be tethered. I just kept thinking, "This can't be happening. How could we be in this position again?"

I went below to gather whatever essential gear we needed. I began to feel the familiar wave of nausea wash over me, but I continued prying open the cabinets to scoop up important documents, our passports, and the EPIRB. Then my stomach turned, and I ran up the steps just in time to puke the little water I had drunk into the rope locker at the top of the companionway.

At that moment, Jim yelled to me, "Mario, I need a knife. I can't get these lines untangled." In the midst of my heaving, I held up my index finger to indicate that I'd do that as soon as I finished puking. He said, "I know you're sick, but I need that knife now. I can't hold on much longer."

"Sorry, Jim. I'm on it."

There was no time to feel sorry for myself. I knew that as soon as I went below deck, I would get sick again. I took a deep breath and started down the stairs. I searched for the box cutter that we had used earlier when nausea hit again, and I began to wretch. The toolbox was still submerged in the foul water. I had to dip my hands into the green gunk, digging through the rusted, slime-filled box to find another utility knife. When I found one, it was rusted shut. I fiddled with it for a while and finally got the blade to come out. But then I couldn't get it to recede. The nausea and dizziness became unbearable, and I ran for the stairs. Once on deck I got sick again, but there was nothing left inside to come up. The dry heaves gripped my entire body as I continued on my way to Jim. I lay on my belly as he did earlier and crawled toward him. He just looked at me with pity as he took the knife from my outstretched hand.

Somehow Jim got the dinghy into the water and dragged it to the stern of the boat. He tied a rope to one grab handle and handed me a tether to tie to the second handle. The waves were slamming the dinghy against the keel of the boat as he attempted to detach the outboard from the two by four that we rigged up the night before. We got the outboard onto the deck and were trying to attach it to the dinghy. Given our earlier experience with the pontoon boat, however, Jim feared that the continued battering it was taking against the keel might puncture the dinghy. As a result, he decided that it would be best to move it to the port side of the boat, where we could affix the outboard motor without the sailboat pounding down upon it. When he unhooked the tether, Sogno was lifted up and pulled away. At that same moment, the other tie line snapped; the two boats began to drift apart.

We froze, both dumbfounded as the scene unfolded. I was on Sogno, and Jim was on the dinghy being pulled away by the swells. He was without a life jacket, paddles, or motor in the midst of 20-foot seas. He was 10 to 15 feet away in mere seconds. All I could think was that this was the end; we would literally drift apart and never see each other again. He couldn't jump in the water for fear of the sharks. I was terrified; I was sure that we would both die apart from each other. Then he snapped out of it. With no oars to aid him, he began to paddle with both hands and yelled for me to throw him a line. I ran to the winches to find a rope that was not completely tangled in the twisted metal of the

Bimini top. Jim saw me struggling to pull the lines free and shouted, "Take your time to get it untangled. You'll get it. Don't panic."

It seemed to take forever. I found a knot of rope, and I began pulling at it to loosen the lines. Once I had gotten enough of it free, I wrapped it around my arm so that I could throw it to him. I had never been a good athlete, and my throwing arm invited lots of taunts and jeers when I was in high school. I knew that my lack of aim would be a challenge when I made the toss. It took all of my concentration; it had to be done correctly. I had no choice. "OK, here it comes Jim, I hope it reaches you."

As I tossed the line to him, a swell knocked the dinghy into the port side of the sailboat. He grabbed the line and quickly secured it. I couldn't believe that it worked. We breathed a momentary sigh of relief; we were back together again.

CHAPTER 23

The prospect of going out into the ocean in our eight-foot dinghy left me cold. We needed to have a back-up plan. I remembered that we had an inflatable life raft stored in one of the lockers. I went to the bench seat on the deck of the sailboat to pull it out. Should anything worse happen, at least we wouldn't be tossed into the water without hope. The storage compartment was spacious and deep. There was plenty of room to store the raft. However, the opening to the locker was narrower than the chamber itself. In order to get the raft in or out, the rectangular canvas bag in which it was encased had to be positioned at just the right angle.

The raft weighed over 100 pounds. In my weakened state, I was struggling to lift it far enough to clear the opening of the locker. With the little strength I had left, I yanked and pulled, but it kept falling back into the compartment.

Finally, using two hands, I got a grip on it and heaved it up onto the rim of the locker. I had done it. The raft was balanced on the edge of the storage locker, and all I had to do was get a bit of leverage to maneuver it out completely. Before I could even take a breath, the fiberglass deck seat slammed onto my head, and the raft fell back down into the locker. It felt as if my head had just been split apart. I was already aching from dehydration and tension; the blow knocked the wind out of me. I almost gave up at that point, but my survival mode kicked back into gear. I knew that I had to get the life raft out of the locker and onto the dinghy. There was no other option but to get it out by myself because Jim was working on getting the outboard motor working. I lifted up the seat once again and leaned my entire upper body down into the locker, balancing my waist at the opening. The cabinet was nearly three feet deep. With my torso dangling into the compartment, I grabbed hold of the raft and hugged it close to my chest. Then I carefully inched my way up and out of the locker. Once I reached the opening, I managed to twist it so that it caught the edge. Then, with all my remaining strength, I pulled it up from the bottom, and it broke free.

The next task was to lift the lifeboat onto the dinghy without capsizing it. I had to time it so that the dinghy was up on a crest of a wave when I released it to Jim, who was waiting to grab it from me. We both watched the waves lift and lower the boat; then, Jim shouted, "now!" As I released it, Jim grabbed it and set it down in the dinghy. Thankfully, it worked with no major trauma.

We still had to attach the outboard motor, and it was still on the deck. Jim had tied a line to the engine and wrapped it around a winch that would carry most of its weight. My job was to lower the motor onto the dinghy slowly. Jim would then grab it and affix it to its mount. With the seas continuing to toss us around, it was challenging to coordinate the hand-off. I lowered it bit by bit until it was at arm's length. Jim reached out to get a hold of it and told me to release the motor. As I did so, the dinghy was thrown against the side of Sogno by a huge swell. The blades of the propeller knocked into Jim's forehead, and he was momentarily dazed. Blood began to flow from the gash it had left. I wasn't sure how badly he was hurt, but there was blood was everywhere, dripping down his face and into his mouth.

"Oh, my God! Jim, are you all right? Your head, you cut your head!"

After the initial shock and pain subsided, Jim reassured me that he was fine. Of course, I understood him well enough to know that he could be lying in order to keep me from worrying.

"I'm fine. Really, I'm fine. I just can't see through all the blood."

As he wiped the blood from his forehead, I could see the cut, which continued to bleed profusely.

"Jim, it looks really deep. You may need stitches."

"No, no, we just have to get off the boat. Besides, there's no one here to stitch me up, unless you want to give it a try?"

"Not funny, Jim. Are you sure you're all right?"

"Yes, yes. OK, let's try it again. Hoist the motor up with the winch, and we'll wait for another opening."

The next attempt worked. A swell lifted the dinghy while I gently let the motor down onto it. Jim held it in place as he affixed it to the mount. After he attached the outboard onto the dinghy, Jim came back onto Sogno. He went below to what used to be the captain's cabin in order to search for our foul weather gear. It was just where he had left it, hanging in the shower compartment. He instructed me to put mine on.

"The reefs are pretty sharp. If we capsize, these will keep us warm and protect us from getting slashed on the coral."

"Honestly? Jim, they're coated with algae and slime. They smell disgusting!"

"We're going to need the protection, Mario. We don't know how long we will be out there."

"Yeah, I know. You're right. It just sucks, like everything else we've gone through in the last 24 hours!"

"Make sure you put on some dry pants underneath. They will help to keep you warm and add another layer of protection."

All I was wearing up to that point were swim trunks and a tee shirt. The only dry pants I could find were Captain Bob's khakis, and his waist was at least 46 inches compared to my 30 inches. If our situation weren't so dire, it would have been comical. I folded the extra 16 inches around my waist and held it in place while I carefully slid the foul weather gear over the pants. The gear was dank and scummy. The bottoms had four months of saltwater muck on them, and the putrid odor made my stomach turn. Sliding my arms and legs into the cold, slimy rubber was disgusting. I lay back on the bunk to put on my boots, and they slipped right on because they were coated with viscous goo. I knew this was the right thing to do to protect us from further harm, but my stomach was turning as I zipped up my jacket. It was all so absurd; I just couldn't believe this was happening.

With the outboard ready to go and all of our essential gear in plastic garbage bags, Jim and I took our final leave of Sogno. Jim hopped into the dinghy first and tried to hold it steady for me. He was always looking out for me, trying to take care of me, and making sure that I always had everything I needed. That has never changed, and none of that was lost on me. I looked at him and nodded, then jumped into the boat. As Jim held the dinghy in place, his fingers were partially submerged in the water.

"Ouch! What the hell was that?"

"What? What happened?" I asked.

"Something bit me! Look, my fingers are bleeding," Jim responded.

"Great! Do they have piranhas here too?" I joked ironically.

We were getting punchy and laughed a bit. Jim then

told me to cut the lines to free us from the boat. I took out the utility knife and sliced away at the only line holding us in. With the rocking of the boat and waves slamming us together, I had trouble keeping hold of the rope. It kept slipping out of my grip. I caught hold of it once again, and I cut and cut, but it just wouldn't slice through. Jim said, "Sure! When you want to cut them, they're strong as hell, but when you need them to be strong, they snap."

CHAPTER 24

I finally cut through the line and we swiftly drifted away. Jim engaged the outboard motor and headed parallel to the shoreline in search of a harbor. It felt as if we were finally free as we both looked back at Sogno. She had almost killed us for the second time. It seemed as if the boat was cursed. I know that sounds superstitious or just plain crazy, but there was a dark energy surrounding everything that had to do with her. Jean Pierre felt it as well; he called her "the devil boat." So I was glad to get away from her and leave all that pain behind us. I just wanted to get to dry land and go back home.

Our relief of being free from the evil aura of Sogno did not last for long. The reality of our situation was beginning to hit us. Dinghies are not meant to be in high seas because they can easily flip over. Jim sat with his hand on the motor, keeping watch on what was in front of us; I faced him from the bow of the dinghy and watched what was coming from behind. The waves poured into the boat but I was ready with a bucket to bail the water. At times it seemed like a never-ending battle but it kept me busy. I didn't have time to worry about our safety. We had to do whatever was needed to get to shore. We were both very alert and we seemed to be dodging the huge breaks in the waves pretty well.

"Where are we heading, Jim?"

"I really don't know. I figure that if we head down the coast there will be a port somewhere."

"Who knew that we would need the GPS more than Jean Pierre?" I grumbled. "At least he had a real powerboat with huge engines."

"I'm sure he is working on getting someone out here to rescue us."

"Well, I hope they get here soon!"

I knew that we couldn't go straight to shore because the Devil's Backbone, the huge coral reef, stretched for miles along the coastline. After a bit of motoring, Jim noticed a microwave tower in the far distance and we hoped that there would be a harbor or an inlet there. With a definite destination in view, we aimed for the tower. We were silent as we motored along the coastline. We were both scared and wondered what would happen next. However, there was no room for addressing our fears; we had to forge ahead.

I'm not sure how long we were motoring, but it seemed like hours. The swells created 20-foot walls rising all around us. We could see land so clearly when we were at the crest of a wave. But the valley between them was ominous; walls of gray-blue ocean seemed to push inward towards us. I was claustrophobic being surrounded by the sea, hoping that none of the waves would break and come tumbling down on us. We forged on as the sun got lower in the sky. When we reached the microwave tower, we realized that it was further inland than it had appeared. We were both deflated; there was no port in sight. Jim looked at me and said, "Ok, so there's no harbor here, but this part of the island is populated. There are a lot of houses right along the shoreline."

"What are you suggesting, Jim? That we should head to shore right here?"

"I don't know. I don't know how much fuel we have

left, and I don't want to be stranded out here without power."

I nodded. "It looks like we're losing daylight too. Do you recall from the maps if we're even close to a harbor?"

"No, I don't. It may literally be a shot in the dark. What do you think we should do, Mario?"

"Well, at least there are houses here. Most of this island is uninhabited, right? If we wait too long we might be stranded with no fuel and no one to help us. Where the hell is the Coast Guard? It's been hours since we sent the SOS signal."

"I don't know. But you're right; maybe we should try to cross the reef here. At least someone might see us and send for help," Jim responded.

"Jim, do you think we can survive crossing the Devil's Backbone?"

"We have to, Mario, we will. I know we will," he said with determination.

We looked out at the reef that stretched for miles in either direction; the waves were crashing down upon it with force. But beyond the area of turbulence, we saw calmer waters that were just inside the reef. There were beautiful white sand beaches with homes looking out over the ocean. We knew what we had to do, so we silently shifted course, keeping our eyes fixed upon the gathering surge around us. We dodged numerous waves as we headed toward shore, but the reef was still ahead. The color of the water changed from deep blue to a crystal clear aquamarine. We were heading into shallower waters. It was almost as if we were tiptoeing over the angry waves, hoping not to be noticed.

As we got closer to the Devil's Backbone, the churning waters became more and more violent. Waves were crashing onto each other with greater force. It looked like we were in a white water rafting route as we were tossed, pushed, and pulled in all different directions. The sound was thundering all around us and we had to shout to be heard. We had made it to the Devil's Backbone and now it was time to cross over.

We braced ourselves for the trial that lay ahead. Jim tried to time our crossing with the break of the waves. He studied them like a surfer waiting for the perfect swell at just the right moment. With little warning, he made his move. He came at it from an angle and tried to ride the top of a huge breaking wave. It was coming at us from behind. He tried to rev the motor to get some speed, but it wasn't powerful enough. As we crested the wave, we felt it begin to buckle beneath us. The dinghy was tossed about like a leaf in the wind and there was nothing to keep us steady. Water was coming at us from every direction but we were still afloat. We thought we might just make it when another surge hit us from the side and crashed directly into us. We were flipped over and pounded under the surf; everything in the dinghy went flying through the air and into the sea, including us.

It all happened in the blink of an eye. The rush of the breaking water pushed at me from multiple directions. I was completely disoriented. I opened my eyes and all I could see was white water swirling around me; it was coming in at me from all sides. My heart was beating rapidly; I couldn't breathe. I desperately tried to get back to the surface for air, but I couldn't tell which way was up. I could no longer see the dinghy. I thrashed about and paddled as hard as I could, trying to figure out which direction would lead me to the surface. Then I noticed the direction the bubbles were moving in and followed them. I used my upper body to propel my way up, only to find myself under the capsized dinghy.

The surf was still churning and there were no air pockets under the dinghy. I dove down but couldn't get much distance; it felt like something was holding me back. I worked my way back up to the surface and once again came up under the dinghy. I was running out of oxygen and I needed to get my head above the water immediately. I dove down a final time and tried to go deeper so as to clear the boat. I emerged with my head bouncing on the rubber pontoon, still under water. The surface was either to my left or my right. I had a 50-50 chance of getting it right. I took a chance and made a decision. Thankfully, I came up right beside the outboard motor. Gasping for air, I heard Jim frantically yelling my name; he had begun to panic when he didn't see me. He tried to look for me but his efforts were fruitless. He dove below but saw nothing but white water. It was so turbulent that he had trouble staying afloat without hanging on to the dinghy. After several failed attempts, he just held on and shouted for me. When he finally saw me, he cried out with relief.

"Oh my God, Mario, I thought you were gone! Are you all right? Just hang on."

When I could finally speak, I responded, "Yeah, I'm just trying to catch my breath."

Jim instructed, "Mario, get on the wave side of the dinghy so that we can be pushed toward the shore." But I began to wiggle around in a frenzy. Something was wrong.

"Jim, I can't move my legs. I don't know what's happening!"

"Do you have any pain? Can you feel them?"

"No pain, I can move my feet. It feels like something is strangling me."

As I thrashed about, I realized that the ropes and gas line were tangled around my legs and waist. I couldn't break free. When we capsized, the lines got caught in the propeller of the motor, wrapped around my legs, and pulled tight. I was trapped. That is why I had so much trouble getting up to the surface when we were thrown overboard. In addition to being tethered to the dinghy motor, I could only use my arms to swim. With the raging waters pushing me in all directions, it was a losing battle. I gasped for air as the swells continued to break over my face. I was having trouble catching my breath through each hit from the crashing waves. Thankfully, with Jim's help, I was finally able to break free of the lines.

Both Jim and I were in shock; the reality of what we had just survived began to sink in. We had been pounded into the reef under the tumultuous waters. Our bodies were slammed against the rocks and dead coral like rag dolls. Had it not been for our foul weather gear, we would have suffered serious lacerations. There was only a moment to absorb the fact that we had survived with minor injuries. But it wasn't over yet. The shoreline was still several miles away.

We managed to hang on to the dinghy and began to calm down. We knew that we had to think rationally in order to survive. There were roughly two miles to go before we reached the shore. We hoped that the waves would eventually push us further into land. As we looked at each other Jim asked,

"Are you doing OK, Mario?"

"Yeah, I'm fine. I finally caught my breath and I don't hurt too much. How are you doing?"

"Good, a little shell-shocked, but good. Let's just get to those houses on shore."

"OK, let's just keep kicking."

Firm in our resolve, we began to kick our legs and push the dinghy toward shore. We were still in the midst of the reef and were surrounded with white water. A few minutes later, we saw some of the white garbage bags that I had filled floating to the surface. "There's all our stuff," I thought and, without thinking, I let go of the dinghy and swam to grab the closest bag. Our identification and all of our important documents were in one of them; I needed to retrieve them. I grabbed the bag no more than 15 feet from the boat, and felt a momentary sense of accomplishment but, once I had it in hand, I thought, "are you crazy Mario? You could have been caught in the reef and not been able to get to the boat."

I could feel my heart racing as I tried to swim back to the dinghy. The waves continued to crash upon me, and I realized how reckless I was being. I was already fatigued from the past 24 hours of seasickness and dehydration. I had used a significant amount of my remaining strength struggling to get to the surface after we had capsized. It was obvious that my determination overcame my ability to reason. I was fighting the stormy waters to get back. In our preparations to abandon Sogno, neither of us thought to put on life jackets. I'm not a particularly pious person, but I recall looking up to the sky and crying out in anger, "What the hell have you done to us?"

Of course, that resulted in a mouth full of salt water from a wave crashing into my face. "Thanks!" I replied.

When I finally reached the dinghy, I was angry with myself. I vowed not to take further risks. Then Jim spotted another one of the bags. I knew that it contained my coveted Nikon camera. It was my baby and I had already lost one on our voyage the previous November. It was his turn to be reckless, so he let go of the boat and swam to retrieve it. He got it in no time and started heading back to me, but the waves fought him as well. I could see him struggling and at one point I feared that he would not be able to get back. He was kicking and paddling forward but the currents were pushing him to the side. When he finally got to the dinghy we both exhaled with relief. What the hell were we thinking? Hadn't we taken enough risks with our lives? What is so important that we had to put ourselves in harm's way once again? Everything else is replaceable; our lives are not.

CHAPTER 25

It got quiet for a long time; the only sound was from the crashing waves. Time passed very slowly. To keep alert, I focused on a house that was particularly grand and beautiful. I concentrated on making it there. Meanwhile, Jim began to see dark shadows beneath him, and his fear mounted. There were aggressive sharks swimming around Sogno when we abandoned her. We were not more than a mile away from there. Could there be sharks near us? Everything was a blur as we floated above the ominous dark images. He kept his eyes focused below and scanned the waters to spot any of those shadows coming closer. He thought, "Damn it! What do we do if they come after us? Jean Pierre said they were black sharks. I wonder if they'll attack if we're just swimming by?"

He decided not to share his concern with me because he didn't want to frighten me. He was in survival mode, and his adrenaline was pumping. It had not even occurred to me to be worried about sharks. I was concentrating so hard on getting us to land that nothing else mattered. The black shadows appeared more and more frequently, and Jim was bracing himself to alert me. Then, all of a sudden, we smacked into a massive ridge of rocks and dead coral that seemed to come out of nowhere. Once again, we were momentarily immobilized. The crashing waves pounded us against the sharp edges of the reef and stone. We tried desperately to keep hold of our raft. If we lost hold of it, we would not survive the swim to shore. After getting banged up and knocked about against the reef, we used the dead coral as leverage and pushed off of it to get back into deeper water. I was so grateful that Jim had been adamant about the thick rubber boots and foul weather gear. Without that protection, our bodies would have been slashed many times over. Instead, we were simply bruised from the impact of each hit. But we wouldn't notice the bruising for hours.

We were both so fatigued and desperate to be onshore. I didn't know how much longer I could keep it up. That house seemed much closer than it actually was. Then we heard the blades of the Coast Guard helicopter roar above us. We were beyond relieved. We turned and waved to signal them, but they passed right by us. It didn't make sense; we had the EPIRB with us, and we were confident that they had gotten a lock on its signal. They missed us even though we were wearing our bright yellow foul weather gear. The strong winds and the high seas created whitecaps on the waves, making it extremely difficult for them to see us. We both felt a bit desperate at that moment. It looked like they were heading in the direction of the abandoned boat. We just hoped that they would circle back around to rescue us.

After that, there was more silence between us. We were both trying desperately to remain hopeful and vigilant, but each disappointment chipped away at our determination. As time passed, we were both getting weaker. Amidst the sound of the waves and the surf, we continued checking in with one another to make sure that we were alert. After so much time submerged in the sea, our body temperatures were getting lower, and we began to shiver. We had been in the water for approximately two hours. Although it was warm for a refreshing swim, it was still about 20 degrees below normal body temperature. We needed to do something so that we wouldn't fall into shock. In an effort to keep each other animated, we brought up silly things or tried to make stupid jokes about our situation.

"People will never believe this!" I said.

"This will make a good book someday!" Jim retorted.

"Wait until Mom and Dad hear what we've gone through. I'm glad they don't know anything about it. They'd freak out."

As we continued our banter, our humor began to get darker. There was a book and later, a movie that came out during the 1980s called Ordinary People. Two brothers get caught in a storm on a sailboat. Only one of them survives and bears the guilt of losing his brother. I had assigned the book for one of the classes I taught and knew the dialogue by heart. I thought of a scene from the movie that shows them struggling during the final moments of their fateful sail. In the movie, they were shouting at each other, so Jim and I mimicked the drama of the film.

"Just hang on!"

"I can't. I can't!"

"Don't let go!"

"I won't, don't you let go!"

Later in the film, the surviving brother, Conrad, meets up with a dear friend. They had met at a psychiatric hospital after their failed suicide attempts. He was feeling lost, and his re-entry into a regular routine was fraught with distress. He needed to capture the comfort and safety of their time together at the hospital. He asked her if she missed being at the hospital where people understood their struggles. But she was in denial and could only talk about how great her life was. When he pressed her on it, she became agitated and anxious. She gets up to leave and tells him that they should have a great Christmas – the best Christmas ever!

Tragically, she later commits suicide during the Christmas holidays. So that's where our banter went next as we exchanged our lines:

"Jim, let's have a great Christmas."

"Let's have the best Christmas ever!" Jim replied.

"We can, you know!" I piped in.

"Yeah, and then we can destroy all of our beloved Christmas ornaments!" Jim said ironically.

"We're not bitter. Not at all," I added.

To this day, when life presents unexpected challenges, we repeat those two lines – "Let's have the best Christmas ever" and "We can, you know." They insert humor into difficult situations while reminding us what we've overcome. This always seems to add a bit of perspective to our current struggles. But as dark as that experience was, it made us laugh a bit as we recognized the absurdity of our predicament. We were literally hanging on for our lives. Our one hope of being rescued just flew right by us. We said anything just to keep up the banter so as not to dwell on the pain and fear.

It got quiet again. I focused on that beautiful beach house on the shore and willed myself to keep going. Each time I began to fade, I would look at the house and try to kick harder. We were so fatigued and so cold that we could hardly imagine getting to shore. At one point, Jim said, "Don't these people ever look out their windows?"

"I know! We are in bright yellow rain gear. How could they miss us?"

"I don't understand why no one has come out to help us," he said hopelessly.

We were growing more and more tired and listless. Though the house was much closer, it still seemed miles away. We had to keep on kicking.

Time passed slowly. Then we looked up and saw we were only about 50 feet from the shore. At this realization, we both got a burst of energy and kicked with all we had left. We knew we had made it, and the shore was within our reach. When we began to feel the sand below our feet, we pushed off it and tried to ride the waves onto the shore. The dinghy hit ground, and we attempted to push it further in and away from the surf. We did it! We had made it safely to shore.

It was at that moment that we finally heard a helicopter overhead, and we waved; it was the Coast Guard at last! They circled around and tried to land on the beach. In the meantime, we labored to get out of the pounding surf—our clothes were soaked with water and filled with sand. Each of my limbs felt like it weighed 100 pounds. Combined with our fatigue, the extra weight made our task even more arduous.

Jim was trying to get the dinghy to hold onto the shore. It had to be flipped upright in order to lodge the motor into the sand. I tried to pull at it, but I had nothing left. We struggled to drag it further onto the beach so it wouldn't wash out to sea.

Suddenly, the beach filled with people. They had finally begun to come out of their houses and gathered around us. I am sure that it was the noise from the helicopter that alerted them. I'm not sure why the helicopter did not land. It hovered above at the other end of the beach and dropped a line. Down came several young Coast Guard officers in dark blue jumpsuits. All at once, I was surrounded by people pressing in on me.

"Are you OK?"

"What happened to you guys?"

"Do you need anything?"

I felt myself start to shake, and all my composure seemed to wash away. I couldn't respond in full sentences, and I felt the tears building behind my eyes. Someone shoved a box of Oreos at me.

"Here, eat these, you need sugar!"

"No, give him some water. He's dehydrated, can't you see?"

I stared at them blankly. It was all so surreal, and I couldn't make sense of all that was coming at me. Then I realized I hadn't seen Jim since the crowd surrounded us. When I looked around for him, I noticed that he was gone; apparently, he was speaking to one of the Coast Guards about our experience. I was given some water and told me to sit down. I tried to take off my soaked gear because I could barely move from its weight.

"No, keep that on. You need to stay warm. The wind is still very strong, and you'll feel colder if you take all that off."

I did what I was told. I couldn't make any more decisions and, although I couldn't quite absorb it all, these strangers were taking good care of me. They were trying desperately to help us. Looking back, I'm humbled by the goodness of people in times of great need. They had no idea who we were, yet they were willing to lend a hand and take care of us.

The Coast Guard came to talk to me and asked me a number of questions regarding the abandonment of Sogno. At first, he seemed to be assessing my mental and emotional state.

"What is your full name?"

"Mario Dell'Olio."

"Where do you live?"

"St. Thomas."

"Are you feeling OK?"

"I think so."

"How long were you in the water?"

"I don't know, a few hours, I think."

"Do you have any serious lacerations from hitting

the coral reef?"

"I can't tell; everything is numb right now."

Once he was convinced that I wasn't seriously injured, he asked where the EPIRP was because it was still giving off the distress signal. I searched for it in the plastic garbage bags that we carried with us. I couldn't stop my fingers from shaking as I handed it over to him. "Here, here it is." He took it from me and shut it off.

"You did the right thing. You kept this with you when you left your boat. The fact that you put on that foul weather gear might very well have saved your lives."

So I suppose that letting go of the dinghy to get that plastic bag wasn't so stupid after all. I couldn't stop shaking; my heart was racing, and I could not think clearly.

"So, what happens next? Are you going to take us back to Nassau? You're not going to leave us here, are you?"

He could hear my voice shaking and saw that I was beginning to panic again.

"Look, you're safe now. Try to breathe, get your heart rate down. I will go speak to my captain and ask what the next steps are. But you need to calm down and rest, OK?"

I nodded my head, knowing he was right. Then he walked over to his commander. After an intense conversation, he returned with the bad news.

"I'm sorry, Mario, but we can't bring you guys back to Nassau with us because we only have 15 minutes of fuel left. We spent so much time looking for you that we used up more than we expected. Your extra weight on the helicopter would mean that we would not have enough fuel for our return." I stared at him in disbelief and exclaimed,

"But what are we supposed to do? We're stranded here with no way to get home!" He sympathized with me but said, "Hey, as long as you are safe from danger, our mission is complete. Look, look at all these people. You will be well taken care of. You are not stranded. I'm sorry, but there is nothing I can do."

With that, he patted me on the shoulder and ran off to board the helicopter.

CHAPTER 26

A man in the crowd had heard the entire exchange and reached out to me. "Hi, Mario. My name is Ralph. I live in that house right there. I assure you that we'll take good care of you. Don't worry about getting back home right now. We need to get you warm and dry."

He led me up a path toward his house; it was the one that I had fixed upon for the last two hours. Ralph's wife, Barbara, came out of the house and told me that Jim was already in the shower and that I should do the same thing to bring up my body temperature. She walked me up to one of their cottages and stopped right outside.

"Let's get your clothes off out here. You've got a lot of sand accumulated in your gear."

I tried to unzip my jacket, but my hands were shaking so badly that I couldn't get a hold of the zipper. I wasn't able to move my fingers nimbly enough to unzip it or get the rest of my clothes off.

Then Barbara began to take the lead and said, "I did this for Jim too, don't be embarrassed. We just need to get you into a good hot shower. OK?"

I nodded my head and let her take care of me. At that point, I didn't care; she was taking charge. I didn't have to think about anything or make any decisions. I was five years old again, and mom was taking care of me. I rested in that comforting thought.

The next thing I recall is that I was in a hot shower, away from all the inquiring people and chaos on the shore. The scene on the beach was a blur to me. I couldn't process all that had happened during the last few hours. The stream of heat from the showerhead felt like a balm on my battered flesh. But I felt dizzy and had to steady myself against the walls of the shower. Having been on the boat or in the water for days, my legs felt wobbly on land. Then my whole body began to shake. The reality of what we had just survived began to sink in. We had been in peril for hours, and our lives had been in great jeopardy. Tears began to mingle with the warm spray on my face, and soon my entire body convulsed as I cried. My anxiety slowly drained away as the hot water warmed my body. We were safe, the trauma was over, and that was all that mattered.

I reluctantly turned the water off and got out of the shower. There was a neatly folded pair of pants and a sweatshirt on the counter waiting for me when I dried myself off. Since Barbara's husband had a waist three times my size, she had found me a pair of her own khaki pants. They looked like they might fit, but when I put them on, I couldn't get the top button fixed. Even so, the zipper went most of the way up, and they stayed on. Thankfully, khakis look similar on both men and women, so you really couldn't tell that I was dressed in women's clothes. We had no shoes except for the boots we wore in the water, so I padded out the door in my bare feet. In the next room, I found Jim sitting on the couch, waiting for me.

He immediately stood, and we fell into each other's arms, holding tightly to one another. It was the first time we had seen each other since we landed on the beach. We held on to each other in silence. After a bit, I just said,

"I want to go home," and I didn't mean St. Thomas. I had had enough of this island adventure. I just wanted to be back on the mainland.

"Yeah, me too. I love you."

"I love you too."

The rest of the evening was surreal. Barbara and Ralph invited us into the main house for dinner. They said it would just be a simple meal, burgers on the grill, salad, and a few sides. I hadn't realized how much I needed to eat; we hadn't eaten in two days. I was famished, and I wolfed down my food without concern for my manners.

Ralph turned to us during the meal and said, "I know that you may not be ready to talk about it, but we are really curious to know what brought you to our shores."

Jim and I exchanged looks. I communicated that I just couldn't, so he began to tell the story. Ralph and Barbara stared in disbelief as Jim recounted the painful details of our sailing adventure. I couldn't help but chime in as the story unfolded, and by the time we finished dinner, Jim and I were as animated as ever. With all the details fresh in our minds, our harrowing tale came to life in vivid detail.

After dinner, the conversation turned to more practical matters. We had to get back to Nassau, and we had very few resources left. In order to give us some badly needed cash, Ralph offered to buy the dinghy from us for $500. We were so grateful and knew that he was just trying to be helpful. Barbara called the only airline that flew out of the local Eleuthera airport and made arrangements for a flight the next morning. With a good meal filling our bellies and the rush of adrenaline subsided, our bodies called for rest. We slowly made our way back to our cottage, where we settled into the deepest sleep we had had in weeks.

CHAPTER 27

The following morning, as we dressed in the same clothes from the night before, we realized that neither of us had shoes. It was an odd predicament, and we weren't sure what to do about it. It was an early morning flight, and the few stores on the island had not opened yet. We assumed that there would be a little shop at the airport where we could pick up a pair of flip-flops or sandals. After a quick breakfast, Ralph and Barbara drove us to the airport.

Eleuthera Airport was smaller than we had imagined. It only had a single runway, and it turned out that there was no shop in which to buy shoes. There were no other options; we would have to board the plane barefoot. Ralph and Barbara wished us well for our return home when they ran into friends of theirs boarding the same flight. Barbara introduced us and gave them a brief synopsis of our story; they were shocked and intrigued. After we thanked our hosts and bid them goodbye, we continued a very spirited conversation with our new friends. Francesco was from Italy and ran a Parmigiano cheese company. His wife, Aliya, was a native Bahamian woman who was as charming and gregarious as could be. She animatedly pressed us for more details of our experiences and future plans.

"We must keep in touch. Your story is fascinating! Where are you staying in Nassau?"

Jim replied, "We're not sure yet. We haven't been in touch with our friend, Jean Pierre since we abandoned Sogno. We stayed with him for a couple of nights at the outset of our trip. But I'm not sure he would be up for that. He was pretty upset and frustrated that last night on the boat."

"Not a problem, boys!" Aliya said, " You will be staying at the Colonial in Nassau. I will take care of everything."

The Colonial is a beautiful luxury hotel in Nassau

with a price tag to match.

"We are pretty short on cash right now, so I really don't think we can stay there, even for one night. But thank you for the offer."

"Oh, Jim, don't you worry. You underestimate my Bahamian powers of persuasion! Leave it all up to me." Jim and I exchanged glances. What had we gotten ourselves into this time?

As we waited for our departure, I looked out to the runway. The plane was tiny, with six or eight rows of seats, and only a few other passengers were traveling with us. The reality of being barefoot struck when we began to board. We had to walk out onto the tarmac without any shoes. The black pavement was already hot in the morning sun. Little pebbles caught in our feet and made it difficult to walk. Jim was in hell. His feet are never out of socks and shoes. I tease him constantly that he has baby feet; even walking on the deck of our boat hurt them. But once we were on board, we settled in for the short trip to Nassau. We actually enjoyed the flight and as well as chatting with our new friends.

Upon landing at Nassau International Airport, the plane taxied and parked a good distance from the terminal. The stairs were wheeled up to the door, and we began to descend. Once again, we would have to walk barefoot on the steaming tarmac to get to the terminal. It just seemed like the fun would never end. After all that we survived, we had to suffer another seemingly ridiculous discomfort. We were relieved to step on the cool floor of the baggage claim area only to discover people staring at us. We were totally unaware of our disheveled appearance. Aliya noticed our discomfort and immediately whisked us away into a waiting taxicab, and we proceeded to the hotel. But our uneasiness intensified when we walked into the elegant lobby of that grand hotel. The looks we received from people at the airport could not compare to those from the guests and staff at the Colonial. The elegant lobby with its marble floors and glittering chandeliers only served to emphasize our unshaven faces, ill-fitting clothes, and dirty bare feet.

Aliya immediately engaged the receptionist in a friendly conversation as she checked us in. She motioned to us to come forward and launched into a fantastic story loosely based on the truth. She told the receptionist that we were photojournalists who had gotten shipwrecked off of Eleuthera and had lost everything but our lives. She told of the dramatic rescue at sea and that our eventual survival was a miracle. The receptionist called over a colleague and who screeched in disbelief. Before we knew it, Aliya had gotten us a complimentary room for that night. We were shocked and thanked her profusely.

"Well, now, we must spend more time with you. Let's go into town after you get settled. I want to show you around."

"The first thing we need to do is go buy shoes. I don't think my burning feet can handle much more of this," I exclaimed.

"Then it's settled. We will meet you in the lobby in 30 minutes. I know the perfect place to go where you won't get taken advantage of. I know the owners well."

We then ambled our way to our room while the other guests and staff continued to gawk at us. But all that was forgotten as we entered our room; it was posh. The king-sized bed was fluffy and soft, and the view was gorgeous. We couldn't believe our good fortune after our latest brush with death. We knew there would be difficulty ahead with regard to the final resolution to our loss, but we gazed at our surroundings with gratitude. We truly felt that each of these moments was a gift that could so easily have been lost.

We met Aliya and Francesco in the lobby and proceeded to walk into town. It was a short walk or would have been if we weren't barefooted. It was early afternoon, and the sun had plenty of time to heat things up. Jim and I were miserable. It felt as if we were walking on hot coals. We passed shop after shop that sold beachwear and shoes; none were good enough for Aliya. We were incredibly grateful to her and her kindness, but we were in pain and just wanted to put something on our feet – anything! At one point we were in front of an historic sight, and she decided that she needed a photo of us.

"My friends will never believe it. I must get some shots of you boys!"

"Sure, no problem. Where do you want us?" I responded.

Jim and I exchanged another knowing glance. This was going to be painful, and it was. It seemed to take forever. She didn't take a quick snapshot.

"Oh, that's not going to work. You're in the shadows. Come out this way, out into the sun. Yes, right there. Wait a minute, let's let these people go by first."

"OK, great. No, move over a bit to the left. Yes, there. That's perfect!"

We ended up moving onto the black pavement because there was a better view. We were posed just perfectly.

Then she asked a passerby to take several photos with her and Francesco joining us. The absurdity of the situation was not lost on any of us except Aliya. I thought, "I guess this is living life to the fullest, breathing in every moment with all its joys and discomforts. And this particular moment just happens to be full of discomfort."

When we finally arrived at the shop, the owner was treated with Aliya's rendition of our plight, and he pressed her for more and more details. I was just happy to be in air conditioning and off the street. Jim and I both purchased pairs of Docksiders, the perfect boat shoe for the newly boat-less couple. They lasted for more than ten years, and for sentimental reasons, I couldn't part with them.

By the time we returned to the hotel later that afternoon, it felt as if we were Aliya's new gay best friends. "After all that you've been through during the last few days, your muscles must be sore. Your bodies must be filled with tension. You must get a massage. I will make an appointment for this evening."

"No, Aliya, it's really not necessary. We are fine."

"I insist, Mario. You boys deserve a bit of pampering!"

She couldn't have been more right. They came directly to our room and set up two massage tables. It was a couple's massage, and we just melted into the tables. It was an incredibly selfish pleasure, and we couldn't have been more grateful. After all that we had experienced during the last 72 hours, we deserved every luxurious moment.

CHAPTER 28

The following day, we boarded our flight to St. Thomas knowing that we had closed the final chapter on our time with Sogno. There would be no more salvage attempts. A salvage company had eventually taken her after she had crashed upon the Devil's Backbone. Because of that, we no longer had any claim on the boat. It was over, and we were ready to move on. Upon our arrival in St. Thomas, Mom and Dad could not have been more demonstrative. Mom hugged me so tightly that I could hardly breathe. They asked what had happened, and we told them the story but left out many of the more terrifying details. Mom recently told me that she realized how harrowing it was for us when she witnessed my manic retelling of the story to one of our friends in St. Thomas. The emotions that she saw me express told her all she needed to know.

After three months in St. Thomas, their visit with us came to an end, but we assured my parents that Jim and I had begun to make plans to return to the mainland permanently. I wanted to leave immediately, but Jim was more practical. There were a few things that we needed to do to get the house in perfect shape. So we spent the following few months getting it ready to put on the market. I continued to paint the unfinished rooms and kept up on the never-ending yard work while Jim fixed broken windows and doors. There was an issue with our septic system, so we had to dig it up and replace it. There was a lot to do before the house was ready for sale. Given all our recent losses, we needed to earn as much money as we could before making the move.

We began to look for jobs back in Connecticut and New York. I sent résumés to schools and churches throughout New England and scoured the internet for job postings for both of us. Near the end of May, I received a call from my alma mater in New England. They had a position open in their Campus Ministry department. Although it was not a music position, I was still very interested. My years at the university were filled with wonderful memories, and I had always dreamed of returning as part of the faculty.

The phone interview went exceptionally well, and they decided to fly me up to meet with the rest of the staff. I was a known entity there. In fact, I had sung for their music director for many years, and she wrote a glowing recommendation. The head of Campus Ministry who interviewed me had been there as a young priest when he was newly ordained. I had fond memories of Fr. O'Connor from my days as an undergraduate. When I arrived on campus, he greeted me enthusiastically and gave me the rundown of the day's schedule. Once I met with each of the other campus ministers, I had an appointment at the personnel office. The interviews seemed to be a mere formality, and I was elated.

I had wonderful conversations with each of the staff. I was very much myself and felt quite at home. I shared stories of my happiest experiences while at the university and how my education there influenced much of what I had done in my professional life. One of my interviews was with an affable woman, and as the conversation progressed, it strayed from the duties of the job and my work experience. We began to chat about our personal lives, and she asked if I was married. I told her about Jim, and the many years we had been together. She continued to ask about our relationship when the tenor of the conversation seemed to take an odd turn, and she asked, "Will you be open with the students about being gay?" My antennae went up immediately; this was not a good sign.

"Well, I don't feel the need to wave any flags. I'm not an activist, but I plan to be honest. If anyone asks me, I will share the truth."

She didn't seem to be bothered by my responses, and I went on to my next meeting. Afterward, Fr. O'Connor met with me briefly and informed me that I would not be meeting with the personnel office due to a scheduling conflict and that he would be in touch with me about the position. I was deflated but remained confident that I would be hired. I told him that I truly believed I was meant to be back at the university, and I looked forward to getting his call. With that, I left campus and drove to my parents' home, just one town away.

I sat at the kitchen table with my father. I needed to make a few phone calls, so I opened their address book, and my old business card from Mission Dolores Basilica fell out. I looked at it and laughed. I handed it to Dad. "Hey Pop,

I don't think you need to hang on to this any longer!" He looked at my title as Director of Music and, with his strong Italian accent, declared, "Eh, you got no job. You got no prestige. You got nothing."

I was so taken aback that I audibly gasped. Then I thought to myself, "I am not 16 years old. I have an adult relationship with my father. I need to respond in an appropriate way and tell him how that made me feel."

"Pa, that's not very nice. That just makes me feel worse than I already do."

"Eh, but it's true, you got nothing!"

At that, my 16-year-old self returned. I lowered my head and walked out of the kitchen. I had so many regrets of my own about having left my successful career in San Francisco, not to mention our beautiful home and wonderful friends. Though he was trying to commiserate with me, my father's words served to reinforce all the negative thoughts I carried with me over the last year. Clearly, I needed to make peace with myself before I could fully heal from my self-inflicted wounds. That was a task that would take a concerted effort as well as the passage of time.

It was weeks before I heard from the university again. Fr. O'Connor informed me that they had decided not to fill the position because of budgetary constraints. When I pressed for further explanation, I received conflicting reasons. When I asked why they would have gone through the expense of flying me up from St. Thomas, he had no concrete answer. Then it occurred to me that the conversation regarding my relationship with Jim might have spooked them. It was a Catholic university, and having an openly gay member on the faculty or the Campus Ministry team might have been too much for them. That cut me to my core and I was inconsolable. That would never have happened in a Catholic institution in San Francisco, where I had been completely out in both my church and teaching positions. New England would be a totally different world for Jim and me.

However, I knew that I couldn't give up my search. There were plenty of other schools, and I was sure that I would find the right fit. But I learned a valuable lesson from that experience. I was no longer in San Francisco, where sexual orientation is a non-issue. I needed to be more discrete. After years of living without prejudice, I had to get accustomed to it once again.

CHAPTER 29

Back in St. Thomas, we had completed all of our house repairs. We called the realtor who had sold us the house and asked her to put it up for sale. Our local friends were very sad about the prospect of our leaving. We had become quite close during our short stay on the island, and it would be painful to leave them.

The process of selling the house took much longer than either of us expected. Back in San Francisco, desirable homes would have multiple offers within weeks, and closing would be done in 30 days or less. We were not emotionally prepared for months of waiting. We accepted the first offer because we were anxious to move on. But the appraisal came in below the sale price, so the prospective buyers reduced their offer. After that, they wanted credits for every little thing that they perceived to be wrong with the property. After numerous demands, we let a deadline expire rather than give in one more time. We let the contract fall through and were ready to start all over again.

There was a local woman who loved our house but couldn't afford the initial asking price. Jim and I figured that we could bring the price down significantly and still make more money than with the previous buyers. When we finally got a reasonable deal together, we were thrilled. The closing date was set at 90 days. Even though that seemed like a long time, we were happy to have it settled. But true to our experience of island life, the closing date was delayed two more weeks because there was only one person in the bank who handled closings, and she happened to be on vacation. The slower pace of life on the islands continued to teach us patience right up until our very last moments there.

We sold the SUV to our friend Stanley. His car was on its last leg, and he was so excited to get a car that was barely used. Because of Jim's meticulous cleaning and waxing, the car looked brand new. As we packed up our belongings for the second time in two years, we were dismayed at how the weather had affected everything we owned. The veneer on our dining room table had buckled, and waves appeared on the surface where it had come unglued. Jim and I both love books, and we had hundreds of them. Many were now filled with mold, and the pages had wrinkled and turned brown. Anything that was leather, including shoes, belts, and coats, was covered with blue mold.

Photography has been a lifelong hobby for me. I had walls and walls of framed photographs chronicling our lives together. Due to the high humidity in St. Thomas, many of the photos had stuck to the glass and could not be removed from their frames. Others curled, became brittle, or were just ruined. I couldn't wait to leave that place. In my mind, it had destroyed our dream retirement as well as many of our precious possessions.

During our last few days on the island, we stayed with our friends Maria and Paul. They had a set of rooms that led directly to their pool, which had sweeping views of the cruise ships and St. Thomas harbor. Maria couldn't have been more welcoming as she cooked delicious meals and doted on us. To top it off, they arranged a lovely farewell dinner before our departure. We gathered at a restaurant with walls made of the beautiful local stone and a gorgeous sea view. The table was filled with so many smiling faces. We laughed a lot, and each of our friends shared stories of their crazy experiences on the island over the years. The most valuable things that we took away from our time in St. Thomas were the deep friendships that we made. They carried us through during our most challenging times there.

The long-anticipated day of our departure finally arrived. Thankfully, we were able to get a non-stop flight directly to Connecticut, so Alex had a much more pleasant travel experience. She seemed to gain a sprightly energy from the cool fall temperatures as soon as we arrived. We were greeted with a great welcome from my parents and siblings at the airport in Hartford. On the drive home to my parents' house, we began to feel a much-needed physical and emotional distance from our traumatic experiences in the Caribbean. The leaves displayed their brilliant fall colors, and the brisk October air was filled with the earthy smell of fallen leaves. I took a deep refreshing breath; I was so grateful to be back home. The oppressive heat and humidity of the tropics were miles behind us.

Surrounded by my family, safe and secure in my hometown, I felt a wave of nostalgia. My parents were empty nesters and had plenty of room for us to stay with them. After our recent life-threatening events, it was more than symbolic that I would find comfort living in my childhood home. My sister and her husband offered the extra rooms in their home. We stored our furniture and our many boxes in their basement until we found a home of our own. We had our safety net, and it would keep us afloat until we could get back on our feet.

Even so, none of us imagined that it would take as long as it did. The tech bubble had burst, and recovery was slow, making it difficult for Jim to find a job. Every company seemed to be downsizing or in a hiring freeze. Since the academic year was in full swing, I decided to begin studies for teacher certification in Connecticut. Months were passing by with no income for either of us; we ended up staying with my parents for nearly two years. We were 41 years old, unemployed, living in my parents' basement. It was a truly humbling experience.

Safe and secure in my childhood home, I spent a great deal of time reflecting upon the entire sailing adventure and rescue attempts. I grappled with my inner demons and wrestled with the many regrets I had regarding what I considered to be the poor decisions that led me to flee San

Francisco in search of an easier life. In some ways, I will never fully understand why so many promising aspirations turned into so much pain and hardship.

My memories of the many days at sea, as well as both rescue efforts, are as vivid now as they were 15 years ago. Gratefully, I don't feel the pain and regret today that I did during those first few years following our rescue. At that time, I looked back on our decision to leave our jobs and home in San Francisco with agonizing regret. I chastised myself for trying to run away from my anxiety and for convincing Jim to go along with my crazy idea of living in the Caribbean. I longed for our previous life in San Francisco, confident that we would return to my beloved city soon after a short stay in Connecticut.

As life so often demonstrates, circumstances changed, and we found ourselves on a totally different path. Jim landed a job in downtown New York City with a not-for-profit organization, so I directed my search to the city as well. Within two months, I interviewed with three independent schools in Manhattan. It's highly unusual to have multiple music director positions open at once in the same city. During the interview at the third school, I knew it was the right place for me. The environment was welcoming, and the school had a strong commitment to social justice. The headmistress picked up on the gender-neutral pronouns I used to conceal that I had a husband rather than a wife. She gave me a knowing smile and repeated my very words in her response to me. She let me know that she understood and that I was welcome there.

Jim and I were quite happy to remain near to my family, especially as my parents were getting older. Now that we were gainfully employed, we began the search for our own home. The prices in the city were well beyond our price range, and we had furniture that could fill 3,000 square feet. There was no chance that we would find anything suitable in New York City. We also focused our search on houses that were large enough to accommodate my parents. We found a great old home in walking distance from the city center in White Plains. It was a classic Georgian colonial that needed a great deal of work. Together we had restored and renovated several houses before, and we looked forward to bringing this old house back to its original glory. It would be a labor of love for us, and it's still a work in progress 15 years later.

Soon after purchasing the house, my parents moved in with us. I am truly grateful for the time we spent together during my father's waning years. My nephew lived with us during his college years as well, and that cemented our already strong bond. Matthew is like a son to us. We had three generations living under our roof, and I will always treasure those years. They were filled with sharing our cultural heritage, cooking lessons, and many family celebrations.

Today, I love my teaching and conducting position in New York City. I am content to be in a school for girls and to help them to find their voices and become strong women. I've developed a great love for my students and colleagues during my time there. Without my identity as a choral conductor and teacher while in St. Thomas, I felt lost and without a purpose. I learned that, for me, a major part of being fulfilled is intricately intertwined with my passion for music. It is an overwhelming feeling when a choral piece comes together for the first time; it's like finding the final piece in a puzzle. And when the performance finally comes, it is like the opening of an art exhibit. The young faces before me create a magical energy, a force that flows through me. It is the closest I have come to Nirvana.

I began my job fully embracing the many commitments of a teacher in an independent school in Manhattan. Over time, I raised the bar for my performance groups, started new ones, and pushed myself to take on increasingly greater challenges. Through my drive to learn more and hone my craft, I became a better musician and teacher. Though my life continues to be extremely busy, I am not trying to run away from it all, as I did during my final years in San Francisco. I have learned to balance my commitments a little better, even though there's always more to learn and more to balance.

I suppose what strikes me most about our time in the Caribbean is how amazingly resilient people are. It's hard to imagine going through all that we had without being irreparably broken. More than once, we nearly lost our lives, and the physical and emotional struggle was unlike anything I had ever known. Yes, it broke us, but not beyond repair. When I think back on the most perilous moments of our journey, I am amazed by the strength of my will to survive. I clearly remember being trapped under the dinghy with my legs wrapped up in the lines. There was never a single thought of giving up or letting go. I fought with every fiber of my being to reach the surface.

As we hung off the boat for hours, waiting to be rescued, it never occurred to me to give up, to let go. I suppose that is the beauty of our human psyche – my defense mechanisms kicked into gear and prevented me from giving up or even entertaining that thought. My body and mind viscerally fought to survive. To be clear, I don't know where that strength came from. I can't comprehend why our perilous situation never caused me to lose hope during those final hours in the water. In reality, at any one of those moments, we could have perished. We could have let go of the dinghy due to exhaustion or hypothermia. Sharks were close by, and their very presence placed us in mortal danger. But I believe we would have fought for survival until the very last moment, no matter the ultimate outcome. Our will to live pushed us to beyond our perceived limits.

I never considered myself to be a particularly strong individual. As a young boy, I was always the short, skinny kid who wasn't particularly good at sports. I was taunted relentlessly in middle and high school. Determined to mitigate those encounters, I began to lift weights in order to change my appearance. Although I became stronger and physically fit, my self-image suffered during those formative years. Sadly, the image of weakness remained in my subconscious and negatively affected my ego for many years to come. But all of that was disproved during both parts of our journey. My body and mind were pushed to their limits, but I persevered. I was able to withstand the hypothermia, seasickness, and physical demands of swimming and hanging onto the raft for hours. After all that we went through, I certainly don't think of myself as weak.

During these last 15 years, Jim and I struggled to regain all that we had lost. My nephew Matthew, who lived with us during his college years, told me that he has never known anyone as driven as we are. Perhaps that's because we nearly lost everything and learned how tenuous life could be. In any case, I relish the hard work and the success it has brought us. I never feel more alive than when I'm immersed in a project or working hard toward a new goal.

POSTLUDE

BEYOND
THE
DREAM

CHAPTER
30

More than 15 years later, I sit on the back porch of a beautiful mansion and look out over Long Island Sound. Sailboats peacefully bob in the calm waters, and tiny waves lap up on the sandy shore. Every year, just after Memorial Day weekend, my colleagues and I bring the senior class to Sag Harbor for their final retreat before graduation. During those days, the girls reflect on their high school years and the journey that has led them here. The retreat guides them from reflections on the past to visions of the future. I am collecting my thoughts for a talk I will give about turning points in life – events that completely transform us or prompt us to change course.

As I sip my coffee, I think back on that saga so many years ago. The usual questions pop into my mind. What was the meaning of those struggles? Why did so many things go wrong at once? Was there some sort of message or lesson that we were supposed to learn as a result? I know I must share a part of my story with these young women as they embark on a new and exciting phase in their lives.

My time in the Caribbean remains the most significant turning point in my life. Who I was before that tumultuous year is very different from the man who emerged from that trauma. The emotional crisis that caused me to flee from my life in California led me to re-evaluate the meaning of my life after our experience. Finding meaning in what took place during our painful sailing adventures has taken years. After sailing in one direction for so many years, I believe that I have come about, changed directions. Though I am still driven toward success, it is not the central focus of my life.

As the girls gather around for my talk, I can feel their energy. They quiet down and look to me with anticipation. I take a deep breath and tell them my harrowing story.

Then I continue.

So, what's the point? Why did I tell you this story? I used to believe that God placed trials in our lives to teach us some sort of lesson or help us to grow stronger. That's what I was taught at school. But I don't believe that any longer. It seems to me that a higher power that purposely inflicts pain on people would be quite cruel. One of my least favorite phrases people use when trying to console others is, "It's God's will." If a person believes in a loving God, it would be incongruous to think that God would cause suffering just to teach a lesson. That is counter to all I learned in my theological studies.

The trials and tribulations of life are simply part of the human experience. We experience pain and struggles, but we also celebrate life's joys. As the years have gone by, I realize that it's up to me to extract meaning from life's experiences. Only then will I be able to move on from the pain. I don't believe that things happen for a reason. I believe it's up to us to reflect on what happens and then give it meaning. I know that it is up to me to learn from all that happens in my life, from my failures and my successes.

I'm sure that many of you struggled with disappointment as you worked your way through the college application process. Each and every circumstance you experience is an opportunity for learning and growth. Some of those experiences are more

challenging than others, and only you can find meaning in them. If I had chosen to wallow in my sadness, I would have sunk deeper into that pain. That would have made it all the more difficult to move on and become a stronger person.

I pause and gaze at the young women seated around me, and I see that they're riveted. I am so thankful for their presence in my life. Teaching them has kept me grounded and focused on what is most important. I continue to tell them what I learned from my turning point.

My perspective on life was transformed during the years following our trauma. I realize that I value life in a different way than I did before the horrific events of that year. That experience forced me to reflect on what is most important. I can't say that I don't feel anxiety over minor challenges in my life, but I have been able to maintain a more even keel. My relationships with those I hold dear are more precious than ever. In most cases, minor annoyances or arguments don't escalate into crises. The bond that Jim and I share was cemented as we struggled through each life-threatening moment. We were constantly looking out for one another and attuned to each other's needs. As a result, we are now quite covetous of our time together and make sure that we truly talk with each other during our alone time.

There was also one stark realization for me. I know

now that, no matter how much I love him or how much he loves me, each of us had to take care of ourselves. There were many circumstances when we had to find our own strength and resilience: we weren't always able to rely on each other for rescue. I had to use my own knowledge and strength to find a solution. I remember the moment the lines snapped when Jim and I went to recover Sogno. I knew that he might drift far away from me on that dinghy in the stormy sea without a life jacket. I was left stranded on the sailboat that was headed on a collision course with the coral reef. At that moment, there was nothing either of us could do but rely upon our individual intellect and strength. I couldn't give up and cry. I had to think fast and make choices. I had to draw from my own well of knowledge and make calculated decisions.

When I was trapped under the dinghy, Jim wasn't there to protect me. I had to figure it out for myself. I had to use my fortitude and stamina to claw my way to the surface. I couldn't rely upon anyone else at that moment; I had to tap into the power and knowledge within me to get through. The more prepared I was regarding boats and sailing, the more likely I would be to survive and thereby help Jim. The same held true for him. People can only help others if they are strong enough to help themselves. I suppose it's like the airplane announcement says: You need to

put on your own air mask before helping those around you. For me, that remains one of the most difficult lessons I learned.

Jim and I continue to strive for more in life—more knowledge, more skills, more love. We are both life-long learners who want to know how things work or what the deeper meaning may be within a statement or philosophy. We question why things are a given way and try to find alternate solutions to problems we face. We continue to stumble and fall, make decisions that might be too risky, or simply make mistakes. But I know that we will get right back up and move on, stronger than we were before.

Though I was more than a little hesitant, I got back on a sailboat shortly after our return from our recovery efforts in the Bahamas. A friend in St. Thomas invited us on his sailboat for a long sail to Puerto Rico. I recall getting anxious when we found ourselves in shallow waters near a coral reef. But we weren't in the middle of the ocean, land was in clear view, and I knew that we weren't in mortal danger. And though I have no desire to sail across the ocean for any reason, I still enjoy sailing in protected waters. Getting back up on the horse after the fall was essential for me, and that's another important lesson I learned. I can't let fear prevent me from taking action – and neither should you. It's important to take calculated risks and dust ourselves off after

a fall. We owe it to ourselves to give each challenge another try. I am sure that there are many lessons yet to be learned. I fully embrace this life with all its trials and tribulations and look forward to our future, knowing that we have the strength to weather any storm.

Perhaps the most important lesson for me is the simplest of them all. Ordinary pleasures take on greater significance for me now. Perhaps it's just that I realize how fleeting life can be. I have become more aware of the little joys in my daily life, like the first sip of coffee in the morning or a quiet meal with Jim at the end of the day. Of course, there will always be major life events to celebrate, like you graduating in one week. What a great accomplishment! But never forget how precious life is, moment to moment. Take the time to recognize your common and familiar routines and be thankful for them. I'm delighted that you have this time to spend with each other; time together with those we love gives color to our lives. Look around you. These are your sisters. You have traveled together on this journey for at least four years. Take a moment to realize how valuable your time together has been.

I'm grateful that I am alive and here to tell this story. Our journey continues, but I will never forget that year in St. Thomas. My experiences throughout those terrifying and

heartbreaking moments have helped to shape the man I have become, and I am certain they will continue to do so. I look to the future with great optimism because, however, difficult life may be, I know that I will face each challenge with strength. I will come through to the other side with more facets and more cuts to the diamond. Some will have been quite painful. But when they catch the light, they sparkle brilliantly with each facet of my life. I know that I am more valuable because of all that I have overcome and experienced. I bring all of that into each relationship I share, and into all that I do.

There are certainly times in life when we must come about – take a different tack and head in a new direction. Don't be afraid to change course. Because of how Jim and I worked through the trauma, those events became a positive turning point in my life and my vision of the future. My wish for you is that you always find meaning in your struggles and that you continue to get back up, dust off, and resume your journey with greater strength and perspective. Remember, there is always hope, and there is always love.

The girls applaud when I finish, and I ask them to share their own experiences. I watch them, happy and animated, as they discuss turning points in their lives. My mind wanders back to the image of Jim and me, reunited after we came ashore in Eleuthera. After nearly losing each other just hours before, we found great comfort in our tender embrace. A smile spreads across my face because I know, unlike that frightening moment, before we abandoned Sogno for the second time, we will never drift apart.

ACKNOWLEDGMENTS

I would like to thank all those who supported me in the writing of this book. It took many years for me to gain enough perspective to consider this endeavor. Thank you to Mark and Cheryl Brownell who were instrumental in launching us into such an exciting adventure. Thank you to Cheryl for her editing and proofing. Your feedback was essential to my work. Thank you to Eileen Pollack, who took on the task of copy-editing and proofing while working full-time in an extremely demanding job. Your full participation in and your encouragement helped me to believe in this project. Thanks to my nephew, Matthew Roberts, for his graphic expertise and help with the cover design.

To our dear friends in St. Thomas who supported us during that difficult year, you were our foundation when the world rocked all around us. And I extend my deepest thanks to my family and friends who housed us and loved us during our transition back to New York. We couldn't have done it without you. To all who cheered me on during the writing process, many thanks. And lastly, my heart-felt thanks to Jim. His meticulous notes taken on the first leg of this journey sparked numerous memories and helped me to form a more accurate account of our sailing experience. Jim's constructive criticism helped to mold this project and his creativity continues to inspire me.

Photo credit: www.matthewdavidroberts.com

ABOUT THE AUTHOR

Dr. Dell'Olio has published two books. Coming About: Life In the Balance and Body And Soul. He is presently querying his third novel, and writing the history of his immigrant parent's love story. As chair of the music department and ethics teacher at an independent school for girls in Manhattan, Mario Dell'Olio conducts the Concert and Chamber Choirs, and is responsible for all Liturgical celebrations for the Lower, Middle and Upper Schools. He leads the Choirs on international and domestic concert tours and has released numerous albums on iTunes and Amazon. com. Dr. Dell'Olio was director of music at Mission Dolores Basilica in San Francisco, California, from 1990-2000. Dr. Dell'Olio holds a Doctor of Sacred Music, a Master of Music in Vocal Performance, and a Masters in Religious Education. He also holds a degree in Psychology. He pursued postgraduate work in Theology at the Pontifical Gregorian University, Rome, Italy. www.mariodellolio.com

CPSIA information can be obtained
at www.ICGtesting.com
Printed in the USA
LVHW022043160721
692932LV00008B/446

9 780692 120781